Praise for *Practice Getting Rich*

Now, please read carefully what these top very important successful people and great achievers are saying about *Practice Getting Rich for a Better Life*.

"*Practice Getting Rich for a Better Life* is a practical guide filled with the tools to create wealth, from the inside out, which is how you get lasting success. I highly recommend you get a copy or two!"

> – **Dr. Terri Levine**, best selling author, including "*Turbo Charge: How to Transform Your Business as a Heart-repreneur®*", speaker, radio host, business coach, and consulting expert.

"*This fast-moving, inspirational book is loaded with great ideas, any one of which can take you from rags to riches.*"

> – **Brian Tracy**, author of "*Getting Rich in America*"

"*Eye-opening and enlightening. Rémi argues that much of our lives are ruled by unconscious stories, good and bad, but that by becoming consciously aware of the cues that trigger our behaviors and the rewards they provide, we can transform bad practices into good ones. I strongly recommend reading* **Practice Getting Rich for a Better Life**, *as it can help you in truly getting rich!*"

> – **Dr. Joe Vitale**, author of "*Zero Limits*" and "*The Miracle*", featured in the movie: *The Secret*

"*I absolutely loved this book,* **Practice Getting Rich for a Better Life**. *It's beautifully written and filled with such wisdom.*"

> – **Raymond Aaron**, author of "*Double Your Income Doing What You Love*" and co-author of "*Chicken Soup for the Parent's Soul*"

"Every now and then, I read a book that truly inspires me. This is exactly what Rémi has achieved with *Practice Getting Rich for a Better Life*."

> – **Peggy McColl**, *New York Times* Best Selling Author

"It's essential and instructive to share what you've learned in life with others, and Rémi does this in an interesting way in this compelling book, *Practice Getting Rich for a Better Life*."

> – **Dr. Nido Qubein**, president of High Point University, author of several books, and speaker on leadership, communication and sales.

"*If you are ready to get rich in a practical way, read **Practice Getting Rich for a Better Life**.*"

> – Greg S. Reid, Author, *Think and Grow Rich* Series

"*Rémi teaches that as long as you do not change your inner world to direct it toward a consciousness of success, abundance, prosperity, and wealth, you will not experience success, abundance, prosperity, and wealth in your life. Read **Practice Getting Rich for a Better Life** to know how to do it!*"

> – **Ray Vincent**, author and motivational speaker

Practice
Getting
Rich for a Better Life

HOW TO CREATE THE LIFE YOU WANT

RÉMI WOGNIN

Published by
Hasmark Publishing
www.hasmarkpublishing.com

Permission should be addressed in writing to Rémi Wognin at
support@practicegettingrich.com.

Editor: Blue Orchard
deb@blueorchard.ca

Book Design: Anne Karklins
annekarklins@gmail.com

ISBN 13: 978-1-989161-29-6
ISBN 10: 1989161294

This work is dedicated to my father, Vangah Kacou Etienne,
my mother, Nogbou Dokoh Florence Louise Christine,
and my brothers and sisters for your unconditional love!

Table of Contents

Acknowledgements

I am grateful for all the people, entities, and events that have helped me to realize that success, abundance, prosperity, and wealth come first from within. Therefore, I truly, truly believe that every Human Being can experience success, abundance, prosperity, and wealth because that is the will of the Universe or God: "Beloved, I pray that in every way you may prosper and enjoy good health, as your soul also prospers" (*3 John 1:2*, Berean Study Bible), moreover we deserve it.

"John answered and said,
A man can receive nothing, except it be given him from heaven."
(*John 3:27*, King James Bible).

"While we look not at the things which are seen, but at the things which are not seen: For the things which are seen are temporal; but the things which are not seen are eternal."
(*2 Corinthians 4:18*, King James Bible).

"Jesus said unto him, if you can believe,
all things are possible to him that believes."
(*Mark 9:23*, King James 2000 Bible).

Introduction

You are finally holding in your hands a practical system that delivers tangible results. Although the title of this book speaks of getting rich, the techniques and methods taught in this book can help you in all areas of your life: Health, peace, joy, love, relationships, etc. "For as he thinks within himself, so he is ..." (*Proverbs 23:7*, New American Standard Bible). I remember a client who had suicidal thoughts after the sudden death of her father; by applying the same techniques explained in this writing, she resumed her taste for life.

Your life up to this point is the result of your thoughts, which build stories, and these thoughts have been received consciously or unconsciously from the outside, through other individuals, from the environment, or even from you. If you do not do anything to change and control your way of thinking right now, in a few months or years from now, you will be the result of the thoughts that you now have, voluntarily or involuntarily. It is sometimes very difficult to understand and accept this concept, and yet it is an obvious reality. Since birth, we have been so used to looking outside of ourselves only, into the physical world, to create or achieve results that we have missed evidence of this reality. Unfortunately, stable and lasting results come first from within – from the mind.

This book will help you in a practical way to take control of your thoughts to achieve the results you want in all areas of your life.

All my life had been based on an unknown story written in advance unconsciously by my environment, my surroundings, and myself. I always wanted the best for myself and for others. However, despite all that I did, it was as if some force somewhere gave me different results from what I really wanted. Sometimes, everything started perfectly well and, then, after a while, everything mysteriously crumbled like a house of cards before my eyes.

I did not understand what was happening to me. I had very good results, but these results did not really correspond to what I wanted. They did not meet my desires. I had the opportunity to work for great companies with very good salaries; however, something in me always told me that I was better than what I was producing. All this looked like an invisible prison. I did not feel in control of my own destiny. There was limitation to everything I did and everything I got. It was as if I was born to be cloistered in a cage or in a certain class of the population and that, despite all that I would do, I could never get out of it. There was no light on my horizon, no long-term hope. This situation was so intense that it created in me the desire to seek a solution to live the life of my dreams.

I remembered very well that in elementary school I often asked myself the question, "what can I do today to have a better life tomorrow?" since I saw people around me with things that I did not have and my parents couldn't afford. During the Christmas holidays, when the other children received their modern gifts from department stores, my friends and I went bare-chested and barefoot in garbage dumps under the sun or in the rain to look for metal debris, as well as piles and old thrown torches to build our toys, which were usually cars.

At one point, I felt that I was not born into the right family because I had the idea that you had to be born into a rich family to become rich or have money to get more money.

As a choirboy at the Catholic school, I often prayed for a better life, but I did not know if my prayers were answered. Then, over time, I adapted to the situation I was living without trying to get more.

Later, I thought diplomas were the solution; I had a lot of diplomas, especially high degrees. I also thought that professional certifications were the solution. I had many professional, international level certifications in my field; in some areas, I was an expert. However, the quest for a supreme solution still existed inside me and rankled me as an incurable disease.

People envied me, but inside, I felt deeply that I was not yet where I needed to be, and I was not yet producing what I should.

As curious as it may be, I often told people that I did not come to earth to follow others, but to do something extraordinary, yet I did not know what that was.

I did not accept at all the idea that God created us to live in poverty, scarcity, and limitation during this life on earth. I thought 'God is good and the giver of plenty'. I tried, as well as tested, a lot of things. Unfortunately, the results never satisfied my deep desire.

It was only when I discovered that I was unconsciously holding within myself a story different from the one I wanted, and when I began to write a new story for the life I wanted, that my results started changing to align with my desires. From that moment, I started to get results that fit the life I wanted.

Today, I have cars for all four seasons. I have cars for spring, summer, fall, and winter as some people have clothes for each season. I just gave a car to my son. If, just two or three years ago, someone had told me that I would live this life, I would not have believed it. During this process, I applied such powerful principles that I decided to share them with everyone.

In this book, I am going to share the practical methods and techniques I used to get the results I have now.

Whether you already live the life you want, or not, this book will help you!

Some authors make success very difficult to learn and apply. I think for myself that it is not at all complicated; it's just a matter of everyday practice like learning to walk or drive a car. It is not just enough to know the methods and techniques associated with the principles of success, but also to apply them systematically in all the circumstances until the desired results are obtained.

The concepts of success, abundance, prosperity, and wealth developed in the Holy Bible, as well as the theories and philosophies proposed by Napoleon Hill, Wallace D. Wattles, and many others, prove that our way of thinking conditions our life, our future, and the results we achieve. Unfortunately, in practice, some people cannot get the results they want. Despite reading many books, participating in various seminars or trainings, these people still cannot achieve the desired results they deserve.

Let's analyze together some of the Holy Bible verses below and the questions they raise:

"But seek ye first the kingdom of God, and his righteousness; and all these things shall be added unto you"(*Matthew 6:33*, King James Bible).

The question that arises here is: What can I do to seek the kingdom of God?

"Jesus said to him, because you have seen me, you have believed; blessed are those who have not seen, and yet have believed" *(John 20:29,* Berean Study Bible).

How can we develop the belief in what we have not seen yet?

"Therefore I tell you, whatever you ask in prayer, believe that you have received it, and it will be yours" (*Mark 11:24,* Berean Study Bible).

How can we ask appropriately while praying?

The Holy Bible, like many other scriptures, speaks of belief and faith. Unfortunately for most of us, no one has taught us how to develop belief and faith.

Is belief just belief in God?

Is faith just faith in God?

"Rejoice always, pray without ceasing, in everything give thanks; for this is the will of God in Christ Jesus for you" (*1 Thessalonians 5:16-18,* New American Standard Bible).

How do we develop gratitude, especially gratitude for what is not yet visible to the five senses?

"Whatever the mind can conceive and believe, the mind can achieve" (*Napoleon Hill*).

How do we use the mind to conceive and believe what we want?

"There is a thinking stuff from which all things are made, and which, in its original state, permeates, penetrates, and fills the interspaces of the universe. A thought in this substance produces the thing that is imaged by thought" (*Wallace D. Wattles*).

How do we put a thought in that substance?

Most people think that wealth is created from the outside. For this, they work very hard on the outside to try to create wealth. Based on this conditioning, some people get results, but these results are still short-lived.

When I study what is written above, I observe that wealth is first spiritual and it is based on faith and belief, then the external result is only a reflection of the inner thought. This is what this book puts into practice.

When talking about wealth, each person has their own idea of what is normal; some people immediately think of money. Yes, money is an integral part of wealth, however, for me; wealth is more encompassing – spiritual, mental, and physical. It includes everything an individual needs for spiritual, mental, and physical development, as well as a rewarding life that includes peace, love, joy, abundance, prosperity, wealth, health, safety, a lot of money, and the blessings of God.

There is no order in this list; therefore, you can choose the order that suits you. In fact, you can create a totally different list; because you are a creator, created in the image of the Divine Creator as stated in the Holy Bible:"Then God said, "Let Us make man in Our image, after Our likeness, to rule over the fish of the sea and the birds of the air, over the livestock, and over all the earth itself and every creature that crawls upon it". So God created man in His own image; in the image of God He created him; male and female He created them. God blessed them and said to them, "Be fruitful and multiply, and fill the earth and subdue it; rule over the fish of the sea and the birds of the air and every creature that crawls upon the earth" (*Genesis 1:26-28*, Berean Study Bible).

In the following, I use the word God; however, you can replace this word by any other word or expression with which you are comfortable, for example, 'Universe', 'Being deep', 'Divine Creator', 'Infinite intelligence', etc.

Several books have been written about the accumulation of wealth, yet most of them focus solely on the external aspect of wealth acquisition. You cannot acquire wealth for long or consistently using only external physical forces.

We must recognize that the physical world is created by the mind so that, to change our results in the physical world, we must first change the way we think.

All wealth comes from within – spirit. This book teaches you step-by-step to combine external and internal actions to create stable wealth. I will show you a very simple technique to create multiple sources of income.

Chapter 1

Who Are You? Identify Your Story!

Before any profound and productive change, it is crucial to know where we are. By creating a balance sheet of our current situation and then, from that point of reference, deciding where we want to go. In my experience, this exercise is the best way to make lasting changes that bring exceptional results.

Note that it is not enough to just change and announce to the world that we are changing to be fashionable – that is only a facade. Here, your life is at stake; therefore, be serious and realistic. We change to move from an unsatisfactory or improving stage or situation, to a better one.

I have to tell you that I had the privilege and the opportunity to work for very large companies. Therefore, I saw a lot of changes. Some changes were appropriate, but others were really a facade. As soon as these types of changes were announced, I saw the flaws; it took only a few months for these flaws to be visible to everyone. Then, we were told of other changes as well as the change in the senior management of the company.

A real change is made to move forward with pleasure towards a better environment than before the change.

Identify Your Story

Identifying your story is very simple; just review your past, look at your past results, and then ask yourself two questions about each result:

- Why did you perform the actions that led you to this result?

- What was the main reason that motivated you to take the actions that led you to this result?

Sometimes you had to do something that was not your own initiative; however, the person or organization who encouraged you to take the actions to get the result had probably given the reason, motivation, or 'why'.

Let's take an example: I met a gentleman who told me that he encouraged all his children to become a police officer because he thought that, at retirement, they would receive a good pension. There is no harm in becoming a police officer, or in practicing any trade or profession. The problem I see here is the consciousness that guides us to let an organization, a government, or an individual decide our future. In the case of the government, for example, a change in a government's policy is enough to put your financial future at risk; there have been several cases in many countries. Certainly, unions can react against a government decision, but nothing usually stops a particular government.

You can undoubtedly choose the job or the profession of your choice; however, the point of advice that I strongly suggest is to use your free time to create a business in order to be financially independent and, thus, to control your financial future yourself.

As we observe, sometimes the intention is clear and unclouded. At other times, the reason is less clear; nevertheless, in general, on the analysis of several results, it is very easy to identify the reason. I often tell people who consult me that to know what a person thinks about most of the time; you just have to observe his or her results. You just have to observe your results and you will discover your dominant thoughts.

In doing this balance-sheet exercise, you should try to establish a list that you will come back to often in order to better analyze your results in-depth and make the necessary corrections. You will find on this book's website, a free sheet that can help you to identify your story.

Another approach is to take a week or a month to systematically write down most of the repetitive ideas and thoughts that come to mind, as well as the reasons that drive you to perform actions. This exercise is about recognizing your inner dialogue and using it to improve your life. You must continue this process several days in succession and then create a list. The analysis of this list will also allow you to know who you are and your story. A free sheet available on this book's website will help you with this exercise.

I had done this exercise with one person and the results were very striking; we had observed together that what he did when he joined a group could only bring him problems with the law. Indeed, in just a few years within this group, he had a criminal record.

This process is like playing a movie about your past. Undeniably, there is always a story behind everything we do; it is after having identified this story that we can enter into an approach to modify it or rewrite it to obtain different results for a better life and, thus, to achieve more wealth.

It is very important to identify where we are because, to change, we must first identify the elements to change or improve; from the analysis of our history, we can identify the elements to improve and this knowledge allows us to create our new life – a better life.

When we look at people who find it difficult to improve their lives, we note that they are using new principles of success on an old internal story, so that they reproduce the same results from the past over and over again.

We spend many years of our life in school learning to work for others, generally as an employee. We do not even ask ourselves whether there is another way to create wealth and financial security for ourselves, our family, and those we love. At the end of schooling, if we have the opportunity to find a job, we work for years and then, from time-to-time, the idea comes to mind to create our own business. Unfortunately, even if we manage to create a business, it cannot provide us with the expected wealth, because we operate this business with the mentality of an employee, which is why most people whom, after starting their own business, encounter problems along the line, resulting in the closure of this business after a few years.

Let me be clear here again; there is nothing wrong with being an excellent employee. Please do not misunderstand. As an employee, you have to work excellently as if you were the owner of the organization for which you work. This attitude will help you move faster in the organization.

In fact, even before creating a business, one must first create within oneself a culture and a consciousness of success, abundance, prosperity, and wealth, as it is written in the Holy Bible: "But seek ye first the kingdom of God, and his righteousness; and all these things shall be added unto you" (*Matthew 6:33*, King James Bible). And, "For as he thinks within himself, so he is" (*Proverbs 23:7*, New American Standard Bible).

To succeed in any business, you always have to work both in the mind and in the physical world. Unfortunately, most of us focus only on the physical world; that's why we get results that are not representative of what we want.

Most people's story is like mine: You had to go to school to get the best degree. Find a good job in government or in a very good organization and get rich. Certainly, some people have become rich using this idea. However, evidence indicates that these people do not control the source of wealth. Therefore, at any time, they can lose it – whatever the quality of their work.

I had these diplomas, I had the opportunity to work for very large organizations with a comfortable salary, but I felt a sense of insecurity in the long-run.

At one point, I made the decision to apply the methods, techniques, and principles taught in this book. I had a business idea. In a few months, I made the decision to stop working as an employee when I had received enough income to take care of my family and myself. The feeling of insecurity disappeared like magic.

Use the methods I present in this book in a repetitive and systematic way to become mathematically rich and to have control over your life, that of your family, and the people you love.

I can tell you my experience; I can tell you what to do; however, nothing beats your own experience – the joy of your own effort, and the enjoyment of your own results by the use of the success principles of the mind.

Please, do this experiment for yourself; to be your own witness of the extraordinary results of the powers of thought. Combine your inner powers, your emotion, gratitude, and faith, then direct it all to any purpose in your life and you will have results mathematically; it is just the law and the principles of the success of the mind in action.

Identify your story and rewrite it to change your life!

Chapter 2

Use the Power of Decision

What is the main goal in your life?

You must certainly use the power of decision to create your dream life.

At this point, you have clearly identified the internal speech or inner talk that has led you to the results you now have. From now on, you will write a new story, or a new goal, that you will install in your mind so that this new story will guide you to a new life – a better life.

When writing the story of your new life, remember that you have no limits. As stated in the Holy Bible: "Jesus said unto him, if you can believe, all things are possible to him that believes" (*Mark 9:23*, King James 2000 Bible). Therefore, we know that everything is possible and allowed; the only limit you have is the one you impose upon yourself, or the one you allow the environment and other people to impose upon you by your own negligence.

The starting point towards achieving any goal is decision. Decision is very powerful, if supported by an unwavering determination to achieve the desired goal. Hesitation has no place in the pursuit of getting rich.

The Holy Bible teaches us that a hesitant person cannot hope for anything, or obtain anything from the divine. Indeed, "but he must ask in faith, without doubting, because he who doubts is like a wave of the sea, blown and tossed by the wind. That man should not expect to receive anything from the Lord. He is a double-minded man, unstable in all his ways" (*James 1: 6-8*, Berean Study Bible).

Here are the main steps to describe your best life – your goal:

- First, decide that you really want this new life and that you are determined to have it.
- Write ten to twenty positive advantages or reasons why you want that goal or that new life (you will read them to motivate yourself when doubts and negative thoughts creep in).
- Write or describe in detail what you call your new life or your future life.
- Refine the description of your future life until it perfectly reflects your ultimate goal in this life.
- Do not hesitate to add all possible details; for you are the master, the responsible, and the conscious architect of your future life.
- Be precise. There is a difference between the phrase "I make money every month," which is vague, and the phrase "I receive more than $100,000 a month," which is more specific and verifiable.
- Use this description in the visualization and affirmation techniques that we will discuss later on in a repetitive way until the desired goal is achieved.

To succeed in this process of internal and external transformation, we must forget or ignore our past and current condition. The Holy Bible says: "Do not call to mind the former things, or ponder things of the past" (*Isaiah 43:18*, New American Standard Bible). Our past, that is to say, our ancient story will try by all means within its power to impose itself as soon as it finds out that a new story is trying to erase it or reduce its influence in your life. Certainly, it will try for many days or months to sabotage your efforts to improve.

It will use apparent facts to dissuade you; it will use events, entities, and individuals in your environment to deter you; at least now, you are aware and you know that it will do so and you will not be distracted by it until your new story takes over in your inner world.

That is why we must be vigilant at all times by controlling our thoughts, actions, words, and especially our emotions. At first, it may seem difficult, after a few weeks all this will be easy, just like a breeze. Everyone has been there so do not be surprised; instead, be pleased to discover that "the old you" is trying to fight by all means in its power to prevent you from installing "the new you".

Here are some negative ideas that may arise in your mind on your personal development journey, as well as suggestions for eliminating them. Actually, there is no right answer; every response that keeps the negative away is great.

Negative idea: You do not need to create a new life because the life you lead now is already enough. There is no point in improving yourself further.

Suggested answer: Regardless of our current level, we can always produce better and be better than we are right now. The Universe, as well as all that it contains, are in a dynamic of perpetual expansion and motion. In this dynamic, nothing stays still, so if you do nothing to be better than what you are today; in reality, you do not stay the same person, you regress. You will not discover it immediately – you will discover it only a few years later. For example, your needs change and evolve – you have to face it; your organism is constantly changing and that requires resources to keep it in excellent condition then, and onward.

Negative idea: This does not work for you. You have read this book many times; you have done the suggested exercises for several months and nothing changes for you.

Suggested answer: What was imprinted in your subconscious mind, and which allows you to produce the results you have now, took a long time to develop. Indeed, it is your old belief that leads you to ask these questions. In the same way, the new life you want to create consciously will also take its time. Nobody has ever mastered a language in a day. Remember that it always takes time to create a profound change in your life.

Know also that the subconscious mind learns through repetition and then, at some point, it will reproduce what it has learned in your behavior in a natural way. You will realize later that you will easily act spontaneously, according to the desire that you wish.

Be patient, remain determined, and persist until you get the best results from your goals, and you too can tell others as a witness that you can undoubtedly, consciously and responsibly, create the life you want.

The duration for the realization in the physical world of the desired outcome varies widely from one individual to another. For example, an individual who has lived in total poverty for a long time will find it more difficult to imagine and even believe in the possibility of living in luxury than someone who already lives in luxury. In addition, remember that each reading of this information expands your consciousness until the principles exposed to it become a normal and integral part of your behavior.

The result will necessarily come because we always harvest what we have sown and, as we know, every seed grows according to its own nature. It is the same thing in the development of a human being. We are different, therefore, the period of obtaining results can also be different and that is what makes life beautiful.

As I already mentioned, you already use these principles in your everyday life; only unconsciously here, all we do is use the same principles, however, in a responsible and deliberate way. So if you've used it unconsciously to get the results you have today, why then will the same technique not work when you use it consciously?

Now that you have read this book, you have the choice to continue either to live the life you have now or to deliberately and responsibly create for yourself the life you want while being in control of what is happening to you.

How do you think you learned the language you speak now? How do you think you have developed the emotion you express about an event? It is through repetition and accumulation.

Negative idea: You do not have the time to devote to visualization and affirmations; you are very busy and overworked.

Suggested answer: Success is achieved by combining the work of internal conditioning and external physical actions. If you limit yourself solely to external activities, you limit the level of success you can achieve.

All successful people in the world spend time every day on their inner spiritual conditioning because they know it's the best way to get the best results and especially the outstanding results.

Do you know a champion who does not condition himself or herself mentally? He or she must see himself or herself on the podium several times in his or her imagination before seeing himself or herself on the physical podium; it is the same for you – you must live your dream life in your own imagination many times before living it in your physical world.

Negative idea: You have already failed several times in several initiatives; why do you think you will succeed in this one?

Suggested answer: How often can a child learning to walk fall before he or she can walk normally; does the child stop learning because he or she just fell? He or she continues with pleasure and sometimes with a smile until he or she learns to walk properly like everyone else. You are capable of more than you believe. Stay in action, always in action, and observe the Universe respond.

Negative idea: Your age, you feel, is too young or too old.

Suggested answer: No one knows in advance the end of this life; use your age as a positive and motivating factor of research for success, whatever your age. Either you have a lot of experience to do what you want better, or you are lucky to have tools at hand to live a better life sooner than others. Therefore, as you note, there are no barriers or limits to the goal of living paradise on this earth now, unlike those who think that one must die to live in paradise.

Negative idea: How can this be possible? You do not have this or you miss it, including money or good health.

Suggested answer: Please remember again this passage, from the Holy Bible: "Jesus said unto him, if you can believe, all things are possible to him that believes" (Mark 9:23, King James 2000 Bible). Therefore, all things are possible to you. The "how" is not your responsibility. Keep in mind that you do not live alone in this Universe, part of your task belongs to you and is your responsibility; the other part belongs to the power that keeps you alive right here and right now. And the "how" is of His domain; all you need to do is to use in your imagination your five senses plus emotion, gratitude, and unwavering faith, until your desire becomes implanted within your subconscious mind and you will be surprised at the results on the outside. Most often, the results appear in the form of internal intuition, events, entities, or people in your environment. When the opportunity arises, you have to act quickly because success likes speed.

We have just answered some questions with some suggestions. Generally, a question contains its answer; you can spend your life eternally asking questions or acting to get better results than you have now.

To help you, repeat the Holy Bible statements below for several days and note how you feel when you repeat them:

- "Do not call to mind the former things, or ponder things of the past" (*Isaiah 43:18*, New American Standard Bible).

- "For behold, I create new heavens and a new earth; and the former things will not be remembered or come to mind" (*Isaiah 65:17*, New American Standard Bible).

- "Beloved, I pray that in every way you may prosper and enjoy good health, as your soul also prospers" (*3 John 1:2*, Berean Study Bible).

Our future is a matter of conscious choices, decisions, and actions, not of chance or luck. The beginning of everything comes from a conscious decision. The powers of thinking and deciding are tools that help us improve our lives.

As soon as I realized that I'm free to think what I want, regardless of my external conditions and environment, I understood at the same time that I had discovered the key or secret of success, happiness, heath, abundance, prosperity, wealth, and all that I want in this world.

When I started to apply these principles, one of the challenges I had was to be precise in my choices and decisions about what I wanted. I thought that being precise meant being demanding of God. This made me vague and broad in my requests, believing that if I was vague, I gave God a lot of choices.

You see, this awareness just proves that I was not in control of my choices and that I wanted to let God or some other entity decide what I want. This attitude can never give you, quickly and precisely, what you want.

For example, if you want to manifest a car, ask for the make, model, color, power, and all the elements that make it unique for you. Contrary to what I thought, the clearer and more precise I was, the faster I got what I wanted – instead of believing that, if I remained vague and broad, I gave God more choice to manifest quickly what I wanted. This is not the case; when you ask something from the Universe, think that you are at a tailor and that you want him or her to create a suit in your size. This dress is unique for you to the point that no one can wear it but you.

Obviously, we are unique, and therefore, be precise and unique in your request to the Universe for quick and unique answers.

I remember in my childhood, that my parents did not have great financial means, but they had the divine grace to have many children. They bought bigger clothes so that each generation of children could wear them. For the school bags, they bought very big bags to be able to use them during several school years. They wanted value for their money. I remember when I was in elementary school, my bag was so big that, when my foot touched it inadvertently, it made a big noise and everyone automatically looked at me. It embarrassed me a lot, and yet I could not change anything.

I was so embarrassed that I began to think and ask myself how to avoid this annoying noise in the classroom and as it is written, "Ask and it will be given to you; seek and you will find; knock and the door will be opened to you. For everyone who asks receives; he who seeks finds; and to him who knocks, the door will be opened" (*Matthew 7:7-8*, Berean Study Bible), I had an idea. At the beginning of the school year, if the teacher did not impose a seating plan on the pupils, I would choose a place at the back of the class and place my big bag against the wall; so when my foot touched my bag, there was no unpleasant noise in the classroom.

This uncomfortable situation has probably also generated in me the ability to take good care of my belongings. When I get something, I keep it for a long time, unlike many other people.

On the other hand, this environment also influenced my attitude to be general, avoid being precise, in order not to embarrass the person to whom I make a request. As a result, I unconsciously transported this consciousness in my requests to the Universe.

However, to approach the Universe regarding what we want, we must be precise and clear about our desire, as a photo is consistent with the person photographed.

In life, we always get everything we think, believe, and feel that we deserve. Start thinking today about: Success, health, abundance, prosperity, wealth, and, especially, a lot of money to experience all this in your physical world.

Most rich people make strategic decisions quickly when they have the necessary information. People who do not succeed are hesitant in their decision.

So, make a firm decision about what you want in this life and do not let anything or anyone distract you from this goal. What do you want that will allow you to say, 'yes, I am so happy to be alive'?

Take serious time to think about it. This is not a light decision; it is a decision about the life you want to live on this planet Earth.

As mentioned above, in reflecting upon your decision, remember that you have unlimited powers and that there is no limit to what you can be, do, or have – the only limit you have is the one you impose on yourself or you let others impose on you.

As we have already stated, write a list of ten to-twenty reasons why you want to get your desire, regardless of your current environment. Ignore your appearance in this current physical world; see in your imagination what you want and you will get it; it is a law of life. When you have doubts, read this list several times with enthusiasm and determination, because nothing stops a determined human being in the faith.

Some people think that you have to choose goals incrementally. For example, you earn $30,000 per year and you want to earn $100,000 per year. These people suggest starting with $50,000 per year first and then, when you get the $50,000 per year, you will ask for $100,000 per year.

We know that, from the moment we begin to think, visualize, affirm, feel, believe, and have gratitude for something we desire, vibrations are emitted to attract what we desire. Therefore, I strongly suggest that you actually ask for what you want based on your current situation; then, when you get it, analyze your situation again and decide what else you want then, and so on.

In the example below, I chose to directly target $100,000 per year as a goal.

Imagine that you currently earn $50,000 yearly and want more than $100,000 yearly. You will, therefore, formulate an affirmation and a visualization scene that proves and persuades you that you already have $100,000 per year.

Your affirmation could be as follows:

Right here and right now, I see, I feel, I believe, I am sure and certain and I have the firm conviction that I receive now more than $100,000 a year. I am so happy; so be it! Thank God and glory to you.

In your imagination, you see $100,000 in your bank account. Touch the money; use your five senses and your emotion around the money;

hear people tell you and congratulate you with joy and surprise that you now have $100,000 in your bank account; hold a party to celebrate your $100,000 in your imaginary bank account.

It is necessary to repeat these visualizations and affirmations with emotion until the result is obtained. Each visualization and affirmation session should last at least thirty minutes in the morning as soon as you wake up as your first activity; then, in the evening, as the last activity before sleeping; as well, during the day, repeat as many affirmations as you can. The goal is that these thoughts become your dominant thoughts to speed up the manifestation in your physical life.

The response to your request will come, as indicated above, from your environment and entities within your environment, including your intuition. So be attentive, observe your environment, and your intuition. You must then act quickly, without delay, by taking actions in the direction of your goal. See the chapter on visualizations and affirmations for more details. However, note that you must always start from where you are, with the means you have, and never stop improving. When the opportunity appears, act promptly.

Motivate yourself with this saying: "We must not put off until tomorrow what we can do the same day". William Clement Stone would say: "DO IT NOW!"

You can observe that, in this example, we do not know how to get what we want. As this is a creative goal, we only know what we desire; therefore, we return to the Universe to enlighten and guide us to the result as stated in the Holy Bible: "The mind of man plans his way, but the LORD directs his steps" (*Proverbs 16: 9*, New American Standard Bible).

In the case of certain objectives, we know what we want, and how to obtain it; in such a case, the approach is different.

I usually group goals in two different groups, namely "creative objective" and "known objective":

1. The "creative objective", that is to say, an objective in which the "how" is unknown;

2. And the goal I call "known objective", in which we know in advance how to proceed because other individuals have already realized a similar goal. Most people limit themselves to this kind of goal.

Creative Objective

For this type of lens, you imagine something that never existed; for example, imagining wireless communication.

In the case of a creative goal, we formulate clearly the affirmation and the visualization scene corresponding to the desired solution, without taking into account the physical world, as if the objective is already realized. We live in this desired outcome in our imagination with faith until we get the final result. During this process, whenever an idea comes to mind, we test it by performing actions in the physical world progressively until the desired goal is achieved. Note that we do actions when an idea crosses our mind because faith without actions is in vain:

- "O foolish man, do you want evidence that faith without deeds is worthless?" (*James 2:20*, Berean Study Bible).
- "As the body without the spirit is dead, so faith without deeds is dead" (*James 2:26*, Berean Study Bible).

Do not confuse the process of manifestation of the creative purpose with the attitude of people who dream in the void. There is always something to do to complete the manifestation process of your goal.

Known Objective

A known objective is a goal that we can see other people achieving; take the case of tennis as an example. If someone wants to become tennis professional, he or she can just follow a few simple steps to achieve his or her goal based on his or her action plan.

Here are some things to consider in achieving a known objective:

- Identify your goals and add a deadline, if necessary;
- Identify the appropriate visualizations and affirmations;
- Identify resources that can help you (the environment, organizations, people, books, etc.);
- Create an action plan;
- Carry out your action plan.

Protect Your Goals

You must absolutely protect your goals. There are so many negative people that, if you reveal your goals before reaching them, they will convince you never to start.

It is normal; they do not even know they're negative. For them, they love you and want to protect you. Recognizing that, already inside of yourself, you have negative thoughts that will try to dissuade you from pursuing your goals. If, in addition to these internal negative thoughts, you add other individuals' negative thoughts, then you create a disabling environment in which you will never reach your goals. Be aware that the chick remains in the egg until it is strong enough to break the egg and make itself visible.

You can talk about light goals, so that the pressure of others can encourage you to reach them; otherwise, you generally keep your goals to yourself until they manifest themselves in the physical world.

An important point to remember is not to be confused about protecting your goals from negative people versus being open with your advisor or an organization that can help and advise you to achieve your goals. I know it very well because as a counselor, when you help a person to create a plan to achieve a specific goal and then subsequently instead of carrying out the action plan to achieve the goal, that individual executes another hidden agenda or plan. In this context, it is very difficult for this person to achieve excellent results.

The tools we use to control negative thoughts are visualization and affirmations with emotion, gratitude, and faith, which are your powers of creation.

Chapter 3

Use Your Powers of Creation

For most of us, the life we lead presently is the result of unconscious visualizations and affirmations. In this chapter, we will learn how to use visualizations and affirmations consciously and deliberately to build a new life exactly like a builder builds a house – he or she chooses suitable materials. This process can take time, depending on your personality.

There is in us an invisible person called The Subconscious, which guides our actions and our behavior. The purpose of this chapter is to program this invisible being so that it guides us in the direction of fulfilling our desires.

I studied math, physics, and logic in exact sciences, so much so, that anything that is not verifiable is worthless to me. Indeed, this science is accurate because it gives exact answers; whatever the environment, and whatever the country in which the experiment is made. Whether you are in Paris, Abidjan, London, Tokyo, Toronto, Berlin, or New Delhi, if you add three plus three, you will obtain the number six as a result. Moreover, this science is accurate no matter what language you use to do the math of three plus three you would still get the number six as a result. One of the limitations of this exact science is that it is based solely on principles that are controllable, can be manipulated, measured, and verifiable by our five external senses in the physical world.

The exact sciences have created many modern inventions and improved our physical knowledge of the Universe. However, as these principles are most often based solely on our five physical senses, this automatically creates physical limitations. For example, we hear some people say that the computer has an infinite power. It makes me laugh a lot because I studied computer science and I even practiced computer science. The computer is unlimited for the person who pronounces the word unlimited. To know if the computer is limited, it is enough to remember that the computer is created in an electronic physical matter that is, itself, limited. So following this reasoning, we see very well that even the memory of the computer will be limited. Today we are talking about cloud computing systems, which are a set of physical systems and therefore limited. All these concepts will change in the future because things evolve in life.

On the other hand, when we talk about the principles of the success of the mind, we also talk about verifiable principles, regardless of the country, culture, language, or region in which the experiment is conducted. Whether "you are in New York City, Bonoua, Moscow, São Paulo, Montreal, Dubai, or Johannesburg, if you follow these principles, which are not based on our five external senses, but based on our imagination using our five internal senses – our feelings that we call emotion as well as gratitude and faith – you would obtain similar results, according to your needs (because every human being has different needs).

The time required for the results of these principles to manifest themselves in the physical world is relative to each individual; however, what is certain is that, no matter where the person does the exercise, the person will get results because we become what we think about most of the time without regard to our culture, our race, or where we live. That is why we must not accuse others of being the cause of our problems – because we can solve them by our thoughts and actions.

The confusion we see with new people who want to learn to apply the principles of the success of the mind is that these people approach this learning with the awareness of the principles related to the five external physical senses. That had been my case until I realized that both worlds: The visible physical world and the invisible world do not use the same principles of success.

Most often, this misunderstanding is what creates confusion and sometimes disappointment. Notwithstanding, in the same way in which the Sun, the Earth, and the other planets remain in equilibrium in their respective places in the Universe, the Infinite intelligence, which has created everything and in who's image the human being was created, responds to the dominant thoughts of human beings and then manifests the results in their physical world.

The principles of the success of the mind really give exceptional results; for example, in the Holy Bible, I did not see the word 'plane'. We see today, the existence of the plane, as well as many other things that did not exist before. All of these things came out of the minds of human beings like you and I who consciously or unconsciously used the same principles of the success of the spirit that we expose in this book.

Do not limit yourself to your physical environment only, because the infinite exists in you and is just waiting for your directives to create a new and richer external world for you.

The Holy Bible tells us not to conform to our present physical world, nor to our present results, but to transform ourselves and improve our lives by renewing our mind. "Do not conform to the pattern of this world, but be transformed by the renewing of your mind. Then you will be able to test and approve what God's will is – his good, pleasing and perfect will" (*Romans 12:2*, New International Version). We will therefore use tools that allow us to renew our mind for a better life.

We have already used some of the techniques that we will see in more detail in this chapter elsewhere in this book, however, in this chapter, we are going give more details and more consistency. The main tools we are going to use are: Affirmations, visualizations, as well as the combination of both, all guided by our imagination.

As we mentioned before, and at different times in other chapters, all the tools and techniques we will use are tools and techniques that every human being already uses naturally – unfortunately, unconsciously and, most often, in a negative way. Take, for example, the imagination; a human being creates nothing without the use of his or her imagination. If you go to a hairdresser, even before he or she begins to style your hair, he or she already has a very precise and clear picture of the style you want in his or her mind. Strangely, all this happens in a fluid and natural way – even though he or she does not realize he or she is using his or her imagination. You do not ask yourself whether you are imagining a style or not.

When the hairdresser finishes his or her work, he or she is certain that he or she has created on your head what he or she saw in his or her imagination; in some cases, he or she is so happy and proud of the work he or she has just finished and you are too.

Let us now take the same example in another way: Imagine that you are going to a hairdresser; he or she starts to do your hair and then, when he or she finishes your hair, he or she shouts saying that he or she has just discovered how to style your hair better than the style he or she has just done. He or she continues saying in fact; I should have done it this way, or that way, and so on. Will you be really happy? The human being does not imagine things or events after; he or she imagines them before. When we imagine something after, it's just to make changes or improvements.

The general procedure is as follows:

- You have an idea or an objective;
- You decide and agree to carry it out with determination;
- You describe a scene with mental images that represents the ideal solution when your goal will be realized;
- You make a statement appropriate to the purpose, which is your affirmation;
- You see and experience the end result in your imagination with your five senses, plus your emotion, as well as with gratitude and faith;
- You repeat your visualizations and affirmations until the desired result is achieved;
- You must remain open-minded and alert at all times by observing your intuition, as well as the events of the physical world that could give you ideas of actions to be performed in the physical world to achieve your goal;
- Repeat from the beginning for your next goal.

How to Create Powerful Affirmations That Work

Positive thinking and affirmations go hand-in-hand and work well together when you have the right affirmations in place.

Affirmations are statements that are focused on a particular goal or outcome. You say these statements as often as possible. Affirmations have been around a long, long time. The idea is to recite the affirmations as often as possible until you believe them. When they become a belief, your subconscious mind picks up on them and creates the situations that reflect your affirmations.

By working with positive affirmations regularly, you create a positive mindset and you start to believe your affirmations. Most people don't get results because they fail to say the affirmations, don't say them enough, don't have affirmations that are well focused, or that are more negative than positive so that they're not really controlling their thoughts.

This is where positive thinking comes in. When you're positive and you recite your affirmations frequently, you're more likely to have success with your affirmations. That's because your positive thoughts will support your affirmations. If you have negative thoughts, then those thoughts will counter your affirmations and make your statements ineffective. You have thousands of thoughts every day. Most of them are negative. And if you're struggling or not happy, then you probably have more negative thoughts than positive.

Affirmation

Create a short, easy-to-remember phrase about your goal already being achieved. Take inspiration from the examples given. This expression must be in the present tense; it must contain, among other things, the following words or expressions: I am, I do, I have, now, etc. It must be recited repeatedly until the manifestation of your desire in the physical world. Each session can last about five, ten, fifteen, thirty minutes or more. As the Holy Bible advises, we must pray unceasingly in joy and gladness: "Rejoice always, pray without ceasing, in everything give thanks; for this is the will of God in Christ Jesus for you" (*1 Thessalonians 5:16-18*, New American Standard Bible).

The thoughts and feeling of your desire already realized must be your dominant vibrational state each day until the manifestation of your desire in the physical world.

To fully understand the creative power of affirmations, see what the Holy Bible tells us: "In the beginning was the Word, and the Word was with God, and the Word was God. He was with God in the beginning. Through him all things were made, and without him nothing was made that has been made" (*John 1: 1-3*, Berean Study Bible).

Therefore, to create; we should use words, affirmations, visualizations, imagination, and emotions with gratitude and faith.

The affirmation should be recited preferably loud enough to hear your own voice. In public, recite your affirmations silently; however, as often as you can, recite them aloud, as if you are talking to another person with conviction.

Another point to know about the affirmation is that it drives us. The words that we recite go into the Universe and then come back to us multiplied for our good if they are positive and constructive, or for our bad if they are negative and destructive.

In fact, the Holy Bible instructs us that the words we recite, and the words we utter into the Universe, will always come back to us with an effect achieving successfully the desired goal; it says:

"For as the rain and the snow come down from heaven, and do not return there without watering the earth and making it bear and sprout, and furnishing seed to the sower and bread to the eater; so will my word be which goes forth from my mouth; it will not return to me empty, without accomplishing what I desire, and without succeeding in the matter for which I sent it. For you will go out with joy and be led forth with peace; the mountains and the hills will break forth into shouts of joy before you, and all the trees of the field will clap their hands" (*Isaiah 55:10-12*, New American Standard Bible).

As we have already mentioned, the recitation of the affirmations must be done aloud, whenever possible.

Do not add negative expressions in the wording of the statement of your affirmation:

• Instead of saying: "I am not sick",
• You must say the following: "I am now in perfect health".

When it comes to health, you have to use affirmations and visualizations while continuing to follow normal prescribed protocols like taking medication until healing.

Think about what you want to change and that means that you focus only on what you want, and not on what you don't want. These phrases exemplify thinking about what you don't want:

• I don't want to be late;
• I don't want to be broke;
• I don't want to be overweight;
• I don't want to be stressed;
• I don't want to be in debt.

As a substitute, focus on what you do want and phrase it positively.

This is a requirement for positive thinking because, when you think about what you don't want, your energy is in the negative. When you think positively about what you do want, your energy is in the positive flow.

When it comes to positive thinking, the emphasis has to be on the positive side on things; so, what you want has to be in the positive tense, otherwise, any positive thinking techniques won't work for you. Change the above statements to what you want, like so:

- I am going to be on time;
- I am rich;
- I am slim and in shape;
- I am always calm and relaxed;
- I now have extra money.

These are new positive statements, and the thought process behind them is positive. This is how you begin to apply positive thinking when you want to create changes in your life.

Formulating Your Affirmation

To formulate your statement, you can draw inspiration from the model below that I often use. You can also add deadlines.

Right here and right now, I see, I feel, I believe, I am sure and certain and I have the firm conviction that…

Indicate here your desire or goal by describing it as already done…

I am so happy!

So be it!

Thank God and glory to you!

Take the case of the example of money:

Right here and right now, I see, I feel, I believe, I am sure and certain and I have the firm conviction that:

I am now receiving over $ per month.

I am so happy!

So be it!

Thank God and glory to you!

Here are other examples of affirmations that you can adapt and use in all areas or circumstances of your life for a better life. The same examples can be used as part of the visualization sessions.

General Affirmations

Every day, in every way, I'm getting better and better (adapted from *Émile Coué*).

I am so happy and grateful now that: **Indicate your desire or purpose here by describing it as already done** (adapted from *Bob Proctor*).

Peace, love, joy, abundance, prosperity, wealth, health, safety, blessings of God!

God, I love you, thank you for my blessings.

I praise and bless everything in my life, thank and glory to you, God.

It's easy and I can (adapted from *Émile Coué*).

Health Affirmations

Every breath purifies and revitalizes my whole body; day-by-day, I am getting better and better.

I feel that I am strong; I feel that I am in perfect health; I feel that I am happy; I feel that everything is fine for me day-by-day.

Every breath I take heals my body.

The joy of the Lord is my strength.

Human Relationship and Love Affirmations

My relationship with X is improving day-by-day.

I love X and X loves me.

God is guiding X to do the right things in every circumstance.

Money Affirmations

I am now receiving over $ a year.

I receive more than $ a month before   (date) .

Business Affirmations

Now, God only attracts to me good people who bring me financial prosperity.

My business prospers day-by-day; I am now receiving more than $ a year.

Employment Affirmations

I always find a job easily, regardless of the conditions of the job market.

Visualization

Visualization is a mental or imaginary scene about a realized goal, an outcome, or the solution to a problem. You create scenes, movies, images, and actions in your mind using your imagination to see yourself being, having, or doing whatever it is that you want, which is your goal. You then play these scenes, movies, images, and actions over and over again daily until the desired result is manifested.

Here is the process:

- Describe, in writing, the perfect and ideal scene of your goal already achieved;
- Memorize this scene;
- Find a quiet and peaceful place;
- Relax completely and forget all your worries;
- Close your eyes;
- Turn your head slightly upwards;
- Be still;
- Breathe slowly and deeply by counting down from ten to one or twenty to one while letting your consciousness follow your breathing and your body relaxes more and more;
- Think for a moment about something that really makes you happy and awakens in you a feeling of joy, love, or gratitude;
- Stay in this pleasant feeling for a few minutes;
- Calmly and confidently direct your consciousness to the scene of your achieved goal in your imagination;
- Live it intensely using your five senses;
- Add the emotion of joy, satisfaction, and gratitude in a feeling of total faith and absolute conviction;
- Stay in this state and repeat the scene in your imagination for at least fifteen minutes, ideally thirty minutes or more;

- Repeat this visualization session two to three times daily until the desired result is achieved.

Sometimes, your attention will be directed to something else, bring your attention quietly back, then continue the rest of the scene.

It is important to do your visualization sessions at least three times a day, because the Holy Bible advises us to pray in the morning, at noon, and in the evening: "Evening, and morning, and at noon, will I pray, and cry aloud: and he shall hear my voice" (*Psalm 55:17*, King James Bible).

Visualization and Affirmation[1]

This technique combines visualization and affirmation. It is one of the most powerful techniques concerning the powers of the creation of the mind. This time, we follow the visualization procedure while reciting the appropriate affirmations in a low voice or aloud, depending on the context. I often use this method. Even during the day when I recite my affirmations, I always inject mental images whenever possible because there is power in our mental images.

Positive Thinking and Affirmations – Working Together

By working with positive affirmations, you eliminate the negative thoughts and you create new positive thoughts because your mind is occupied by what you desire – your goal. Your subconscious then creates new situations in your life based on these thoughts, once you believe them. And that is the challenge. You see, most people create affirmations that they do not really believe. They are often too long and seem too far-fetched, so they give up on them and say they do not work.

To get results with affirmations, they have to be positive, focused on what you want – your goal – in the right tense, easy to remember and you have to support them with regular positive thinking so that you think about why you can succeed instead of why you cannot. Please remember, both are creative, for good or bad.

Too many people use old affirmations from books or affirmations that were created by someone who doesn't know anything about affirmations. Old affirmations are often phrased incorrectly because you simply don't speak that way anymore. Your affirmations should always be in the present

1. On my website (https://remiwognin.com), in Downloads section, you are going to find recordings that can help you during your Visualization and Affirmation sessions.

tense, they should be positive, they should usually be short and simple, and they should focus on what you want, which is the realized desire. Your affirmations should not contain any negative statements.

When you follow these criteria, you'll develop affirmations that are easy to remember, they'll work, and you'll develop positive thinking patterns that lead to even greater success.

Here's an example: If you want to get a job, then create an affirmation that helps you get a job. A good series of affirmations would be:

- I now have my perfect job; I am so happy.
- I am doing the right things to get a job.
- I make the right impression and I've got a terrific new job.
- I am guided to get the best job.

Next, think of the criteria and add that to the affirmation. If you wanted a job that is close to home, then you would say: "I've got a job that's close to home."

If you have a certain salary requirement, add that to the affirmation. Break up the affirmation so that different sections target what you want.

Notice: There are no negative words in the affirmations. This is important because positive affirmations lead to positive thinking, which leads to success.

Now the important part: You have to work with the affirmations every day, throughout the day as often as you can. There is no set number of times that you should say your affirmations. But if you say them only once a day you're not going to get results quickly and it will take a long, long time for you to believe them. The more often you say your affirmations, the more you support them with positive actions and positive thinking, the sooner you'll begin to believe them and the sooner you'll see changes in your life.

Managing Negative Thoughts

Whoever you are, you will always have negative ideas or doubts. The real challenge lies in being aware of them and then preparing yourself to replace them with positive ideas and emotions related to your future goals, seen as if they were already realized; that's what all great champions or personalities do. Otherwise, they would not be champions. It is also the best way to be the master of one's mind and, consequently, one's destiny.

Be responsible and do not let negativity bring you where it wants you to go.

You cannot lead or live the life of your dreams by letting your mind wander and store any idea that settles there. In the same way that a vagabond goes nowhere in his or her life; every human being who has no control over his or her thoughts cannot live the life of his dreams.

Do not think for a minute that there are human beings who have never had negative thoughts or doubts. Even Jesus Christ has been tempted. The Holy Bible said: "Because He Himself suffered when He was tempted, He is able to help those who are being tempted" (*Hebrews 2:18*, Berean Study Bible). Negativity and doubts are an integral part of the normal life of a human being.

The Holy Bible reminds us to be eternally vigilant and to focus our attention solely on our goals as if they were already realized and they will be: "Be sober, be vigilant; because your adversary the devil, as a roaring lion, walks about, seeking whom he may devour" (*1 Peter 5: 8*, King James Bible).

External events will always happen in your life to distract you from your goals, occupy your thoughts; waste your time, and influence your emotions. Do not get distracted by these events; they are just temporary distractions on the way to your assured success.

During any given day, several ideas cross your mind; this is normal, do not be distracted by these. Know that you can only think of one thing at a given moment, even if you feel that a lot of things are occupying your mind. Take the example of the chair – if someone occupies a chair, no one else can sit on it, unless sitting on the person who is already in the chair. Negotiation will be required. As a result, keep your mind constantly occupied with thoughts and images of what you want until it manifests itself in your physical world.

If you find yourself in negativity, you can erase it by repeating several times: Cancel! Cancel! Cancel! Then, immediately substitute mental images of your goals followed by strong motivational affirmations and visualizations.

The Best Times to Influence the Subconscious

In reality, the subconscious can be influenced at any time of the day; nevertheless, we know that any event or idea imbued with emotions easily influences the subconscious. That's why we need to pay close attention to our thoughts and emotions. It is generally recognized that early in the morning, just after waking up, and late in the evening, just before sleep, are the best times during a day to influence the subconscious. We can also add that the vibrations of faith, love, and gratitude influence the subconscious, as well as moments of relaxation or excitement.

Some Examples of Results:

Find a Person

A person who owed me money had left his address and changed his phone number. I had no way of finding him. So I asked myself: How can I find him? Sometime later, I had the idea to use visualization to find him.

So, I began to visualize, imagining that the person was giving me money. I did my visualization sessions without necessarily expecting any-thing special since visualization has now become an integral part of my way of life.

One day, during my travels, I had taken a path by mistake; I did not take this path usually. Instead of turning around, I just told myself that I would continue on the same path.

Arriving at a crossroad, I saw the man waiting on the sidewalk for the red light to cross. As soon as he saw me, he tried to change his path. I parked my car safely and then I ran up to catch him. That's how I got his information, which allowed me to get my money back.

By analyzing this example, I see that I had taken a path inadvertently; on this track, if I had driven faster than expected I would never have seen him. Alternatively, if I rolled too slowly, he would have passed before I arrived at the crossroads and so I would not have met him. Likewise, if I had been delayed by an event or a previous red light, there too, I would never have been able to see him.

The point in this example is to observe that several events have synchronized themselves to guide me and draw him to me so that I met him at the right time in that particular place. Yes, the Universe attracts to us what we think about most of the time.

Then, negative thinking will tell me that it happened just by chance. This kind of negative thinking is correct. I accept that this point of view of this negative thought is not mine; because I note with joy and gratitude that since I use the techniques exposed in this book, there is a lot of chance that goes great for me than before. I, therefore, prefer to continue in the direction of my visualizations and affirmations.

Manifest a Car

I visualized and made affirmations about being in a Jaguar car of a very precise model and color. In the scene I visualized, I saw myself sitting in this car and driving. Then, one day in the physical world, I drove to my mechanic's garage to have him change my tires; when I arrived, I saw a beautiful parked car that looked exactly like the one I had seen in my visualizations; the only difference was the color.

I turned in next to the car and stared at. Then, the mechanic asked me, "Do you like the car? Do you want to buy it?"

I responded, "Yes! How much is it?"

He replied, "It is for a retiree; he wants to sell it quickly." And then he told me the price. As the color did not match my desire, I chose another one that matched exactly the color I wanted. I had managed to negotiate the price to a level I thought reasonable for myself, even if I did not have the amount requested. Note here that I negotiated the price of a car knowing that I did not have the negotiated amount at that moment. To reassure the seller, I gave him a deposit, which I could afford to lose if I could not find the necessary funds. I had made an appointment with the seller in three days at the vehicle registration office. I started making a financial package. An hour before the appointment time, I was running out of money to buy the car, but I had a very strong faith that I would have the car of my dreams. I kept checking my bank account on the Internet. About thirty minutes before the meeting, a transfer went into my bank account, which allowed me to purchase my Jaguar, based on the model and color of my dreams.

In this example, also the negative spirit can come to find reasons, causes, excuses, and questions. However, I prefer to believe that it is my desire that manifests itself and not something else. Remember that the negative spirit can be internal or external so be always vigilant and cautious.

Healing a Trembling Hand

One day, during a real-estate transaction with a client, when I had passed her the pen to complete the engagement sheet, I observed that her hand had suddenly begun to shake abnormally. However, her hand had not shaken during our conversation beforehand.

She was looking at me, telling me that whenever she had to fill out a document in public, her hand began to shake and she did not understand the reason.

I replied that it was not a problem and that I could fill in the document for her. She refused, saying that she wanted to do it herself to familiarize herself with it. I insisted and, finally, she let me fill in the form. For the signature of the document, I asked her to sign because it was a legal document.

At the end of the transaction, I walked briskly to my car to continue my other appointments of the day. At one point, I heard someone's voice calling me back. I stopped to look behind me and I saw her coming towards me, telling me to stop because she had a problem to submit. As I like helping people, I stopped.

When she caught up to me, she started to tell me her story: For more than two years, as soon as she has to fill in a document in public, her hand starts to shake. She had medical check-ups, but the doctors had not found anything and they just asked her to write often; for that, she had almost written a book. She had prayed with pastors at church and everywhere, however, all that changed nothing.

She asked me if I could do anything to help her. I had asked myself the question: How can she know if I could be able to help her? What can show that makes her think I can help her in this situation? I told her that her problem was very simple and easy to solve; it will finish very quickly. I asked her, "What religion do you practice?"

She replied that she was a Christian. I asked for more details and she told me she was Protestant.

I suggested this to her: "Here is what you will do every night as the last thing before you go to bed, and then in the morning as your first activity. It must be done for at least thirty minutes at each session and during the day, when you remember to repeat the affirmations. You must do this practice systematically for at least thirty consecutive days, ideally ninety days. At the end of this period, the problem will disappear or you will have an appreciable relief. In the meantime, stop all other prayers."

Here is the proposed formula:

See yourself in your imagination filling out forms in front of three or four people in a stressful environment; for example: In job interviews, before a judge and lawyers, or in front of police officers.

As you visualize the scene of this stressful environment, repeat, continually, the following statement, which is your affirmation:

- Say thank you God;
- Recite the "Our Father" prayer;
- thank God and glory to you;
- Right here and right now, I see, I feel, I believe, I am sure and certain and I have the firm conviction that I now write perfectly well in public; I am so happy;
- So be it;
- Thank God and glory to you.

I had asked her to practice this technique for three days and to call me to see if there were improvements to be made and also to make sure that she used the technique the right way. By the third day, I had emphasized certain points. Then I asked her to call me back in eight days for follow-up.

I also promised her that I was going to pray for her on my side at the same time.

About three weeks later, when I met her in another setting, I asked her how was her mental conditioning practice. She answered me very happy and with a big smile: Do you not see how happy and resplendent I am? I went to several places and everything went well. It's finished – the problem has disappeared; I am so happy. I had asked her, all the same, to continue for at least thirty days so that the mental anchor was well reinforced.

Note in this story that I had asked a question about her religion because I wanted to build on the belief that she already had to speed up the result, instead of creating a new belief.

Remember what the Holy Bible said about belief: "Jesus said unto him, if you can believe, all things are possible to him that believes" (*Mark 9:23*, King James 2000 Bible).

If the person were not religious, I would change the presentation of visualization and affirmation.

Bird Hunting

Special observation: Note that this hunt is for consumption. It is neither to demonstrate my dexterity in hunting nor to throw away the birds killed. In the same way that some people kill chickens, fish, or other animals for consumption, this hunt was essentially for consumption not for waste.

When I was in elementary school, I used to go to the forest to hunt birds with friends. Generally, I could kill just one or two birds after about two hours of hunting. I asked myself the question: How can I kill more birds? Then, one day, I was alone hunting and I had the idea to do this: When I saw a bird on the branch of a tree, I proceeded as follows: I looked at the position of the bird; I closed my eyes for a few seconds while staring at where I wanted to reach, then opened my eyes and pulled. In less than thirty minutes, I had killed so many birds that I had decided to stop the hunt. I was very surprised and I wondered since then what had happened.

Today, I understand the reason; I was simply using the power of visualization. It is a technique in three stages:

1. Observe the position of the bird in the environment;
2. Visualize for a few seconds in the mind with opened eyes or closed eyes the final destination of the projectile;
3. Shoot quickly.

This technique can be applied or adapted to other areas of activity; as well for hunting as in some sports. If you use it systematically you will observe, statistically, that you will have a high probability of having more success in your favor than otherwise.

Some Techniques to Condition the Subconscious:

Song Technique

Transform your affirmation into songs. Generally, I use the sound of songs that are already familiar to me and that evokes emotion in me – especially emotions of joy or pleasure. Then, I sing this song repeatedly until I get results. You can also invent the sound of the songs you want because you are a creator.

Writing Technique

Hand-write your affirmation ten to twenty times consecutively once a day. This technique influences the subconscious since, while you are writing, you repeat the words silently or aloud. The Holy Bible suggests writing your vision down: "Then the LORD answered me: "Write down this vision and clearly inscribe it on tablets, so that a herald may run with it. For the vision awaits an appointed time; it testifies of the end, and will not lie. Though it lingers, wait for it, since it will surely come and not delay"" (*Habakkuk 2:2-3*, Berean Study Bible).

Mirror Technique

Stand in front of a mirror; look into your eyes and repeat your affirmations for ten, fifteen, or twenty minutes, two or three times a day, because the eyes are the mirror of the soul.

Recording Technique

Record your main affirmations; repeat each ten to twenty times, then constantly listen to this recording at any time. At night time, do it at a low volume until you get the results.

Dream Images Technique

Use a sheet, a notebook, or an electronic file; in it, draw or paste pictures of everything you want in your life; look at this sheet, this notebook, or this file once a day, usually in the evening before falling asleep.

Music Technique[2]

Find inspiring music to play during your visualization and affirmation sessions that will allow you to be more relaxed and thus better able to influence the subconscious.

Of course, you can combine the above techniques, depending on the importance of your goal.

Every idea that is maintained in the mind for a long time automatically manifests itself in our life as objects, events, circumstances, and so on, since the visible is always created by the invisible. It is here that the internal work begins; it is here that we create in our mind abundance, prosperity, wealth, and all that we desire in our life; it will always be visible later in our physical world.

As we have seen previously, we all already do visualization and affirmations; unfortunately, we do them negatively most often, which means that we receive results that are not up to our expectations.

---

2. On my website (https://remiwognin.com), in Downloads section, you are going to find recordings that can help you during your Visualization and Affirmation sessions.

Remember, when a negative event occurs, how long do you think about it? You see images; you hear words; you form words. By staying in this state, other similar events naturally occur in your life.

Using the techniques outlined in this chapter, you will learn to master your visualization and affirmations for a better life.

When I suggest people work with visualization and affirmations, some people automatically want results at the speed of light. Unquestionably, it is possible to have results quickly, but what must be remembered is that the time to have results is the time of God, so it is a perfect time. The Holy Bible says that the result will not delay: "For the vision awaits an appointed time; it testifies of the end, and will not lie. Though it lingers, wait for it, since it will surely come and not delay" (*Habakkuk 2:2*, Berean Study Bible).

Until this point of our life, we are the result of our thoughts. We will become the result of the thoughts we have today and now. Our behavior is guided by our subconscious; therefore, through the practice of visualization and affirmation, we can condition our subconscious so that our future behavior and our results reflect our deep desires.

By doing visualization and affirmation, we put ourselves in a mental disposition with the firm conviction, assurance, and gratitude that what we want to create already exists now and not in the future. We do not take into account facts in the physical world because we want to create a new life from "nothing" as the Divine Creator does.

For example, if we are in a very poor environment and want to create a rich and abundant environment, it is in our interest to ignore this poor environment and visualize only the desired rich environment until that environment manifests itself in our physical environment.

The Duration

The subconscious is influenced by daily repetition of an attitude. One must make visualizations and affirmations incessantly until the desired results are obtained as it is indicated in the Holy Bible: "Rejoice always, pray without ceasing, in everything give thanks; for this is the will of God in Christ Jesus for you" (*1 Thessalonians 5: 16-18*, New American Standard Bible).

As an indication, let's stress that you must spend at least thirty minutes as soon as you wake up in the morning and at least thirty minutes in the evening just before going to bed. Outside these times, always have the image of your realized goal in mind; this image must be accompanied by affirmations. You can also make affirmations in five-minute, ten-minute, or fifteen-minute cycles.

Whether you believe it or not, everything you imagine, visualize, think about, and what you say will manifest one way or another in your life. This is what Napoleon Hill[3] calls to 'transmute our thoughts into their physical equivalent'.

Exercise

This exercise will help you to determine if the daily actions you perform are in line with your secondary objectives and your ultimate goal. Recall that a secondary objective is an objective, the realization of which brings us closer to achieving the ultimate goal. It is, in a way, a sub-objective of the supreme objective. Generally, it is strongly advised to break down any objective into sub-objectives to reach the main objective more easily and quickly; this is the technique of dividing and conquering.

During a day, write down all the tasks and actions you perform to create a list of these tasks and actions. At the end of the day, before going to bed, go back to the list and, for each item in your list, ask yourself three questions:

1. What is the purpose of the item?
2. Does the item correspond to my ultimate goal?
3. Is the item one of the secondary objectives?

Then, you have to cross out all the tasks and actions that do not correspond to neither the secondary objectives nor the supreme goal. Note that I am asking you to cross them out and not delete or remove tasks and actions that do not correspond to the secondary objectives or the ultimate goal, because you can come back later to realize that these items may be useful as part of one of your secondary or ultimate goals in the future.

You must continue this exercise until you reach the point where, in the course of a day, all your tasks and actions are in line with your objectives and working towards the realization of these. You will quickly discover that your tasks and actions will be automatically and naturally oriented towards the accomplishment of your objectives.

---

3. Hill, Napoleon (1937). *Think and Grow Rich*. Chicago, Illinois: Combined Registry Company.

This exercise can also be considered as an exercise of focus, because in life, during a day, many things can seek to distract our attention and use our time. We must therefore be constantly vigilant, often asking whether these events contribute to the achievement of our objectives, and then making the necessary adjustments to carry out only the tasks and actions that guide us towards the achievement of our objectives.

The previous exercise of focus on tasks and daily actions also applies to thoughts that cross our mind during a day. Indeed, during a day, thousands of thoughts cross our mind. We must control these thoughts. Dwell, and focus only on the thoughts that lead us to our goals while automatically canceling those that are not in line with our goals. Since thoughts are creative, if we dwell on thoughts that are not consistent with our goals, we will create things that will not fit our goals.

As in everything else, the beginning will seem difficult for some people; this is normal. Notwithstanding, with practice, everything will become simple and automatic. I know for myself that I constantly ask myself the question: Do my actions, my tasks, and my thoughts match my goals? Then, if it is not the case, I cancel them out and I immediately immerse myself in the image and the feeling of my objectives as being already realized.

Examples of Objectives Seen as Already Realized:

Objective seen as already realized is the final solution you want to be, do, or have in the physical world; that is the final state. That state must not be an intermediate step.

In the example of selling a car, you must put up the sign, "for sale" and advertise normally. However, in your mind, the final image you need to see is, "already sold". There is a difference. People who come to visit or to try the car are an intermediate step. Therefore, these people do not have to be in the final image of the desired solution in your mind.

In the case of renting a house, for example, the sign will say, "for rent", then advertising to rent the house. However, in your mind you must see the display, "already rented".

Your mind hates emptiness; give it the image and the feelings of your objectives as already realized, so that it guides you towards the realization of these objectives.

Please note that in this process of reprogramming your subconscious mind; the key word is 'relax' that's why I use carefully selected recordings as background sound while I'm doing my visualization and affirmation sessions. I advise you to do the same because these sounds talk directly to the subconscious mind, in the same time they relax you, and they have many health benefits. That way you get the fastest results. On my website (https://remiwognin.com) you will find free selected recordings that will help you relax while you are doing your visualization and affirmation sessions.

Chapter 4

Take Action

Visualizations and affirmations without actions in the physical world are like someone who dreams without ever following through on those dreams to something concrete for himself, or herself, or for others. The Holy Bible reminds us that faith without action is in vain: "O foolish man, do you want evidence that faith without deeds is worthless" (*James 2:20*, Berean Study Bible)?

When we undertake actions in the physical world, we take into account verifiable facts of the environment in contrast to visualization and affirmation that are internal actions.

Let me explain: When we visualize our goals fulfilled and repeat affirmations, most often we are endeavoring to create something from nothing – just like our Divine Creator. Since we are creating something completely new, there are no facts to evaluate or analyze.

However, if, for example, you want to buy a car and then resell it, you have a physical item – the car – that you can diligently evaluate and analyze before proceeding. Completing visualizations and affirmations does not negate the need to engage in any business without study or due diligence; negligence has no place in the orderly and disciplined process for financial and personal success that I propose.

This seems contradictory, but it is in this respect that many people who try to use the powers of the mind are mistaken.

When I propose to people how to create wealth, one of the first answers that I always get is, 'I do not have the money to start'. Unlike most people believe, we do not start a business with money only. Money is just one of many elements necessary for the success of a business; unfortunately, our pre-existing conditioning about money and other 'needs', depending on our education or our culture, limit our thinking.

One day, someone said to me: "I do not have all the necessary government approvals yet to start my business." I told him that it's a very good thing because it's an opportunity for him to use his mind to create and run his business. He looked at me very surprised and I repeated to him the same thing again, because that way, as soon as he obtains the authorizations, everything will be easier for him. It is true that it is difficult to understand and believe that everything begins first in the mind; however, it does. All stable wealth begins in the mind.

As no one can stop you from thinking about what you want, therefore nothing can stop you from creating your own wealth by starting in your own mind.

Do not expect to succeed without a single challenge because it is by successfully meeting challenges that you grow. If people give you what you need easily and quickly that is good; but, do not expect people to make your way easier. Some people will consciously create obstacles, but you know that you have the tools to overcome any obstacle.

There will be obstacles and there will be highs; however, know that these happen to everyone and, as the Universe is dynamic, follow this dynamic to move forward until you see the light that is your goals manifested in the physical world.

As written in the Holy Bible, "ask and it will be given to you; seek and you will find; knock and the door will be opened to you. For everyone who asks receives; he who seeks finds; and to him who knocks, the door will be opened" (*Matthew 7: 7-8*, Berean Study Bible).

Therefore, you must never stop asking, searching, or knocking on all doors until you get what you want in your life. You do not have to be afraid of rejection or be ashamed because it's all part of normal life.

Daily Programming

The Morning

When you wake up:

- Fifteen to thirty minutes of visualizations and affirmations.
- Write five to seven main objectives.
- Read aloud the list of activities created the day before and make changes, if necessary.

During the Day

- Repeat affirmations in cycles of five, ten, or fifteen minutes, with the images of the goals for which you are making the affirmations in mind.
- Execute the list of activities created the day before in order of priority. Carry out one activity at a time. If the activities are not complete at the end of the day, continue them the next day, always respecting the order of priority.
- Listen to your intuition, which is God's answer to your desires and act on any idea that creeps in.

The Evening

- In your imagination, review your day; replace the recollection of any bad event with your version of the perfect scenario to create a perfect day.
- Do fifteen to thirty minutes of visualizations and affirmations.
- Rewrite your five-to-seven main objectives.
- Write a list of the main activities to be carried out the next day; add priorities by determining which tasks will bring you to your goal the fastest.

Learn Assiduously

I classify learning in two parts: External learning and internal learning.

External learning is the learning that one receives from a book, a seminar, training, or advisers.

Internal learning refers to the learning that is acquired by controlling and observing one's own attitude in one's everyday behavior in one's work, actions, and experience. We will come back to this kind of learning in more detail in the following chapters.

Here are the cyclical action techniques I use to exercise persistence and strengthen my enthusiasm every day:

- Prepare Spiritually;
- Prepare Mentally;
- Prepare Emotionally;
- Learn;
- Act;
- Evaluate the Results;
- Adjust, if necessary;
- Return to spiritual preparation to begin the cycle again, again, and again.

Prepare Spiritually

We must first realize that our desire comes from a source that is divine and infinite. Here is what the Holy Bible says about divine guidance: "When people do not accept divine guidance, they run wild. But whoever obeys the law is joyful" (*Proverbs 29:18*, New Living Translation). It added: "A Song of ascents. Of Solomon. Unless the LORD builds the house, its builders labor in vain; unless the LORD protects the city, its watchmen stand guard in vain" (*Psalm 127:1*, Berean Study Bible).

This divine source is also abundant and unlimited. Know that: "Whatever you ask for you will receive it; whatever you seek you will find it, and if you knock, it will be opened to you (*Matthew 7: 7-8*, Berean Study Bible). These laws operate without exception and are available to every human being. All durable and stable good comes from the divine world. The Holy Bible tells us: "John answered and said, a man can receive nothing, except it be given him from heaven" (*John 3:27*, King James Bible). Moreover, the Holy Bible said: "But seek ye first the kingdom of God, and his righteousness; and all these things shall be added unto you" (*Matthew 6:33*, King James Bible).

Prepare Mentally

Within our mind, we must consciously build the perfect image of the ideal solution or the ideal scene of what we desire to have in the physical world – even if, for the moment, it is only in the mental world.

In some cases, the image is not possible. In these circumstances, first, describe in writing what you want. Then memorize this writing, which is the ideal situation for the desired solution. Then, repeat this description constantly until you get the results.

Prepare Emotionally

It is important to see intense emotion as the energy that will accelerate the realization of your desire in the physical world. So the more you emit emotion, the faster you will get tangible results.

Feel the emotion of your already realized desire and live it constantly until it manifests itself in the physical world. Here, you have to be careful; it is not a question of thinking that the desire will be realized in the future, but that it has already been realized and now you experience the feeling of joy, pleasure, fulfillment, and liberation of the ideal solution already achieved. See in your mind good friends or important people congratulate you and be in the surprise and joy of your realized desire.

Observe that, at this point, I am not asking you to think about how you will achieve your desire. It's not about thinking about the "how". The Divine, who is omniscient, omnipotent, and omnipresent, knows very well the 'how' and moreover the best 'how'; it is not up to us to tell the Divine how to proceed. The Divine is truly omniscient, omnipotent, and omnipresent; let Him play His part because He is an essential spiritual partner. He knows everything and will present to you the best way. All you need to do now is just to live the emotion of end result of what you desire as a child of the Divine. The holy Bible teaches us that the Universe will give us the best steps – the 'how': "The mind of man plans his way, But the LORD directs his steps" (*Proverbs 16:9*, New American Standard Bible).

While doing all this spiritual, mental, and emotional conditioning, pay close attention to your intuition, which will direct you in the 'how' to achieve your desire. When this intuition comes to mind automatically, take action immediately. Part of the action could be learning – perhaps getting to know the market or the domain. Even if you already know the domain, check that your information and knowledge are up-to-date because things can change quickly, like laws, for example. As one prepares for success, one must learn before moving onto actions, then review those actions, and then make adjustments, if necessary. Continue this exercise until you realize your desire. Remember; the Holy Bible tells us that: "Therefore I tell you, whatever you ask in prayer, believe that you have received it, and it will be yours" (*Mark 11:24*, Berean Study Bible).

Learn

On the importance of learning, let's look at this example together: I had bought a building; a few years later, my neighbor wanted to sell his building. For lack of knowledge and learning, I could not pull together the appropriate financial resources to buy his building. I had used conventional financing techniques, instead of following the ones used by investment experts in real estate.

Now, imagine the opposite case: Instead of using common sense and conventional methods of financing, I had this book on-hand and I used the techniques that are explained here. Then, I hired a seasoned real estate investment expert in my area to set up the transaction. Do you think I would have had better results? Yes, of course. So, remember this: Learning, learning, and always learning. This technique is what I call buying knowledge from an expert or a specialist. This advice is applicable in all areas.

The lesson here is the importance of always working with appropriate advisors or improving one's knowledge by learning the relevant field of activity. This is also why, in all my advice, I emphasize that people are constantly learning in the field where they want to practice.

We often hear from individuals or groups advertising business services and saying that these businesses are not risky. This "risk-free" phrase always makes me smile because, if there were a risk-free business, everyone would do it with their eyes closed. So, beware of this type of business opportunity promotion. Each opportunity comes with risk; however, the risk should not prevent us from undertaking the business. In all business opportunities, one must, identify the risk and then control it to be successful.

In fact, when you have the intuition to do something, learning is an integral part of the actions needed to lead you toward success and the fulfillment of your desires. However, I separate learning from other actions to emphasize that learning is a crucial element in preparing for success because most people think that, because they have an idea, they will execute it with eyes closed, without regard to the environment. Once again, I repeat: We are preparing for success and success requires work and training. All champions train to attain the results we see. Yet, for some mysterious reason, it does not occur to us that, to create our wealth, also takes continuous training, preparation, and learning.

If you take the time to constantly learn and prepare, you will feel that everything becomes easy and automatic. As if it's a natural part of you. When another person sees you in action, he or she will think that it is too easy and there is no effort required. This impression is normal because you have mastered the situation. It is the same thing with great champions. When we see a champion practicing his or her sport, or the activity within his or her favorite field, we think it's too easy, it's too perfect and it's okay. The constant training helps us to improve to become better, better, and better.

Just as champions are constantly working day-after-day to reach a point of excellence, you must also work mentally and physically every day to fulfill your desires for yourself, and those you love

Act

Actions are all the mental and physical activities you do to reach your ultimate goal. For example, if your ultimate goal is wealth accumulation, then your actions should be directed toward creating the services or products that will earn you money when others use them. In this context, your main objective is not the services or the products. A service can be considered as a secondary objective. Personally, I had tested several services before moving forward with the services I offer now.

Evaluate the Results

We are going to discuss the evaluation of results in another chapter. However, here, I place it in context with what I consider a conscientious human being must constantly monitor, analyze, and control – his or her thoughts, his or her words, his or her deeds, and his or her actions – then make adjustments when necessary.

Adjust, If Necessary

The adjustments or correction needed to advance one's life from success to success begins first in the mind, concerning the modification of the image or the mental description of the ideal desire, before automatically propagating itself in the physical world. All levels of your being must be constantly aligned to achieve stable and permanent outstanding results.

You can spend your life focusing on changing the physical world only to realize that it's like building a house of cards on sand; everything will collapse in front of your eyes in a very short time. When this happens, some people panic and then appeal to priests, pastors, or other entities to help them.

By following all these processes, you are mentally and physically moving away from all that is negative and the opposite of the desire you wish to obtain. Avoid contact and communication with negative people, as they will contaminate you with their negativity. Stay constantly in a positive vibration regarding your already realized desire.

Chapter 5

Move Mountains

We have repeatedly mentioned that one of the essential tools for the manifestation of our desires is faith, which is a firm assurance of what we desire and a manifestation of what we do not see: "Now faith is the assurance of what we hope for and the certainty of what we do not see" (*Hebrews 11:1*, Berean Study Bible).

Please, pay close attention to this expression: "The certainty of what we do not see" – this is the key to faith. Therefore, from now on, do not limit yourself to what you see in your life because you can change them using the powers of the mind.

The Holy Bible informs us that faith moves mountains: "Because you have so little faith. He answered. For truly I tell you, if you have faith the size of a mustard seed, you can say to this mountain, move from here to there, and it will move. Nothing will be impossible for you" (*Matthew 17:20*, Berean Study Bible).

We now know that everything is possible with faith, and that faith is not just a pretty word in a scripture or a pretty word to hear, but also and above all, it is a state of consciousness, a vibration of very powerful energy that can really transform our lives and help us create a better life if we know how to use it.

We must have faith in ourselves as a human being with creative powers, like those of the Divine Creator. And, we must have faith in our ability to create whatever we want. The Holy Bible teaches us that whatever we want, we can obtain in faith; therefore there is no limit to what a human being can be, do, or have in his or her life. "If you believe, you will receive whatever you ask in prayer" (*Matthew 21:22*, Berean Study Bible).

As with other things in our life, faith must be developed and nurtured so that it can be powerful and serve us more in fulfilling our desires – our goals.

Developing an attitude of faith requires daily practice because, as we have already mentioned, every thought that you have at any time, either consciously or sub-consciously, creates something in your life and conditions your future.

To develop my faith, the main tools I use are visualizations, affirmations, reading holy or inspirational books like the one you are currently reading, or listening to the audio and video versions of these books, as well as taking action in the physical world.

The Holy Bible instructs us that faith develops through the continuous and repetitive listening of words: "Consequently, faith comes by hearing, and hearing by the word of Christ" (*Romans 10:17*, Berean Study Bible).

Let us take an example: When you visualize and develop statements of affirmation around a desire, then you perform actions to achieve it successfully, what happens? Your confidence in yourself increases; your faith develops, as well as your enthusiasm. You acquire more energy to undertake other more ambitious goals, and so on. This is how you grow on your path towards achieving your ideal future at your own pace; it is really an amazing pleasure.

As we have already stated above, many people think that succeeding in business requires only monetary means. Unfortunately, it is not the case. Success in business includes, among other things, a spiritual, mental, emotional, and physical conditioning to enable you to face and master all the events that can occur on your path to success. Money is just one of many elements to master and control until we reach our goals in the visible world.

I often suggest to people who approach me for advice to have in their mind that they are created in the image of the Creator and that they should recite these Holy Bible verses several times a day for at least thirty consecutive days: "In the beginning was the Word, and the Word was with God, and the Word was God. He was with God in the beginning. Through Him all things were made, and without Him nothing was made that has been made" (*John 1:1-3*, Berean Study Bible). Then, they observe what is happening inside and around them.

Indeed, words are the main tool of the creation of God. Likewise, we, just like God, can use faith, visualizations, and affirmations to create the life we desire.

Even Jesus used just the word and faith in His many healings. He stated, "Blessed are those who believe without seeing": "Jesus said to him, because you have seen me, you have believed; blessed are those who have not seen, and yet have believed" (*John 20:29*, Berean Study Bible). Unfortunately, our education and our environment have conditioned us to believe only in what we see, which, by the way, is very limited. I hope you understand now why people who live only in the physical world lead a limited life.

Let's analyze this example of Jesus' healing together: "After Jesus had entered the house; the blind men came to him. "Do you believe that I am able to do this?" He asked. "Yes, Lord," they answered. Then He touched their eyes and said, 'according to your faith will it be done to you'" (*Matthew 9: 28-29*, Berean Study Bible).

For me, this demonstrates the need for unshakeable faith, both from Jesus and from the blind men. It also shows that this universal power is just waiting for our instruction by the magnitude of our faith and our determination to fulfill all our desires – our goals. Unfortunately, we have not traditionally been educated or trained to communicate with this universal and infinitely creative power; we have therefore allowed our physical world to gain the upper hand in all our businesses and actions.

This was really my case in the past; I went to church to pray with faith in God, Jesus Christ, and all the saints. Then, I left the church and, in my daily actions, I only considered physical facts; under these conditions, you can easily imagine what kind of results I obtained. Of course, I also prayed for things but I did not pray creatively as outlined in this book, and so, again, my results spoke for themselves.

I was even afraid to ask for something material in my prayers because I thought it was a sin to want physical things. Yet, the same Jesus Christ in whom I believe so much turned water into wine and he tells us: "First seek the kingdom and righteousness of God; and all these things will be given to you above" (*Matthew 6:33*, King James Bible).

Again, for me here "all these things" implies that there is no limit to what a human being can be, do, or have in this life. "Righteousness" means we should always be honest and fair in dealing with people and organizations.

So, you can easily imagine now how much the environments and conditionings in which some people like me lived, differed in relation to the use of faith this book describes to fulfill our desires.

Jesus had shown by His miracles of multiplication that God loves success, abundance, prosperity, and wealth. Wherever He went, if there was a lack, He created abundance. Yet, for some surprising, mysterious reasons, it did not occur to me that I could do the same thing to create success, abundance, prosperity, and wealth in my life.

The truth is, that everything we see in the visible Universe is just a small part of what the universe represents. The visible can always be easily modified by the invisible. This is why all the Scriptures say that everything we see or manipulate with our five senses is illusion – because the invisible powers of the mind can easily change them. Indeed, the Holy Bible says, "While we look not at the things which are seen, but at the things which are not seen: For the things which are seen are temporal; but the things which are not seen are eternal" (*2 Corinthians 4:18*, King James Bible). It adds, "For we live by faith, not by sight" (*2 Corinthians 5: 7*, New International Version).

In the same way, our external conditions in life can easily be modified by new thoughts within our minds. All the good things of the modern world that we see around us today have been created from the unseen – the imagination of the human being – including the chair on which you sit.

Therefore, we must never let our current external conditions prevent us from working within our imagination, to create a new external world for ourselves, our loved ones, our family, and the people we love.

When Jesus performed His miracles of multiplication, it was neither for Him alone, nor for His disciples only. He performed them for everyone – for "the multitude", as the Holy Bible says.

To create a better external world for ourselves and our loved ones, we must consistently have a clear picture of what we desire in our mind until this image is transformed or manifested into our outer world as a tangible reality.

Here are some tools to help you to develop your belief:

- Constantly control your thoughts, emotions, beliefs, behavior, and actions.
- Participate in personal development training seminars.
- Read and re-read motivational and self-help books like this book in a repetitive way.
- Listen to motivational and personal development audio[4] and video recordings every day on a recurring basis.
- Have counselors in every important area of your life because the Holy Bible teaches us that: "He that walketh with wise men shall be wise: But a companion of fools shall be destroyed" (*Proverbs 13:20*, King James Bible).
- Rigorously select the people you communicate with often.
- Control your environment.
- Learn new concepts regularly to get better, better, and better.
- Control your negativity and remove or substitute it for what you want as soon as you become aware of it.

Proactively Prepare Affirmations

Anyone can have negative thoughts, for even Jesus had been tempted: "Because he himself suffered when he was tempted, he is able to help those who are being tempted" (*Hebrews 2:18*, Berean Study Bible).

That's why you need to prepare positive statements or affirmations and visualizations that you can immediately use when you feel negative.

Proactively preparing affirmations and visualizations is very important because it is difficult to create a positive affirmation when one feels deeply negative. In a negative state of mind, you cannot be easily inspired positively; it will be difficult for you in this state to create a good positive affirmation or visualization to overcome that negativity. The Holy Bible advises us to be constantly vigilant, because the enemy of our goals may appear at any time: "Be sober, be vigilant; because your adversary the devil, as a roaring lion, walks about, seeking whom he may devour" (*1 Peter 5: 8*, King James Bible).

---

4. On my website (https://remiwognin.com), in Downloads section, you are going to find recordings that can help you during your Visualization and Affirmation sessions.

Control Your Environment

Since our environment conditions our lives and our intelligence, it is important to pay particular attention to it. Sometimes we can change or leave our environment but, at other times, we cannot change it.

We must constantly control everything that enters our environment and then eliminate everything that does not comply with our objectives. This process requires daily work.

You cannot easily develop a positive attitude and unwavering faith in an environment in which all the people around you think negatively and have chronic negative attitudes.

When we cannot leave or change our environment, one of the techniques I advise is to adapt by focusing inwardly regardless of what is happening outside – what Napoleon Hill[5] calls 'positive mental attitude'. Focusing inwardly, on your thoughts, can always free you from outward conditions.

Here is a list of Bible verses that I often use as an affirmation to strengthen my faith:

- "Because everyone born of God overcomes the world. And this is the victory that has overcome the world: our faith" *(1 John 5: 4*, Berean Study Bible).
- "But he must ask in faith, without doubting, because he who doubts is like a wave of the sea, blown and tossed by the wind" *(James 1: 6*, Berean Study Bible).
- "'Truly I tell you', Jesus replied, 'if you have faith and do not doubt, not only will you do what was done to the fig tree, but even if you say to this mountain, be lifted up and thrown into the sea, it will happen. If you believe, you will receive whatever you ask in prayer'" *(Matthew 21: 21-22*, Berean Study Bible).
- "'Have faith in God', Jesus said to them. 'Truly I tell you that if anyone says to this mountain, be lifted up and thrown into the sea, and has no doubt in his heart but believes that it will happen, it will be done for him. Therefore I tell you, whatever you ask in prayer, believe that you have received it, and it will be yours'" *(Mark 11: 22-24*, Berean Study Bible).

5. Hill, Napoleon, Stone, W. Clement (1991). *Success Through A Positive Mental Attitude*, Pocket Books

To people who are like I was – who have faith in God and in Jesus Christ, but who at the same time continue to believe that the poorer you are, the closer you are to God or loved by God – I propose to you to imitate Jesus Christ, or God Himself, in the creation of success, abundance, prosperity, and wealth for the multitude, as the Holy Bible advises us. This imitation of Christ or God does not constitute blasphemy, for it says in the Holy Bible, "Be imitators of God, therefore, as beloved children" (*Ephesians 5: 1*, Berean Study Bible).

If, at any time in our life, we notice or feel that we are missing something, remember at this very moment that we are neglecting to use the powers of the creation of the divine within us. Let us change the situation by using our creative powers.

Refuse poverty, scarcity, or any other form of limitation: In thought, word, deed, and action! Then, watch your life change without outward effort on your part because your subconscious mind has been reprogrammed for: Success, abundance, prosperity, and wealth!

When you feel ready to decide to leave poverty behind, the real question is not 'how can I get out of poverty?' This question contains the word 'poverty', which is associated with scarcity and, therefore, does not represent an attribute of God. The attributes of God include: Power, strength, success, abundance, prosperity, wealth, omnipotence, omnipresence, and omniscience. The real question then is 'what can I do to outwardly manifest in my physical world the abundance, prosperity, and wealth that already exist inside me?' For the kingdom of God already exists within us: "Neither shall they say, see here! Or, see there! For, behold, the kingdom of God is within you" (*Luke 17:21*, American King James Version). In a kingdom, there is no poverty or scarcity when the king is God Himself.

Imitate Jesus Christ

Wherever Jesus found scarcity, poverty, or any lack, He exercised His power of multiplication, abundance, prosperity, and wealth in a masterly way. For instance, at a wedding party in Cana, He transformed water into wine and at a large gathering; He multiplied loaves and fish to feed everyone: "Jesus told the servants, "Fill the jars with water."So they filled them to the brim. "Now draw some out, He said, "And take it to the master of the banquet." They did so, and the master of the banquet tasted the water that had been turned into wine. He did not know where it was from, but the servants who had drawn the water knew. Then he called the bridegroom aside" (*John 2:7-9*, Berean Study Bible).

Observe that Jesus created for Himself and for others. He did not create for Himself alone, nor just for His disciples. We too, in our life, do not need to settle for little, nor to suffer limitations. Like Jesus, let us visualize abundance, prosperity, and wealth without ever being satisfied with crumbs, since we are created in the image of God and can do the same things – not in stress, but in pleasure and joy.

Let us see some examples of Jesus' miracles of multiplication:

- "Have the people sit down, Jesus said. There was plenty of grass in that place, so the men sat down, about five thousand of them. Then Jesus took the loaves and the fish, gave thanks, and distributed to those who were seated as much as they wanted. And when everyone was full, He said to His disciples, gather the pieces that are left over so that nothing will be wasted" (*John 6:10-12*, Berean Study Bible).

- "How many loaves do you have?" Jesus asked. Seven, they replied, and a few small fish. And He directed the crowd to sit down on the ground. Taking the seven loaves and the fish, He gave thanks and broke them. Then He gave them to the disciples, and the disciples gave them to the people. They all ate and were satisfied, and the disciples picked up seven basketfuls of broken pieces that were left over" (*Matthew 15: 34-37*, Berean Study Bible).

I observe in these examples above that when Jesus notes that there is a lack, He does not create 'just enough', He creates more than enough. This proves that He does not content Himself with the little. He produces in abundance what the Holy Bible calls "the pieces that remain" or the "left over". This is very striking for me; it tells me that He is not content with the minimum, as some people want us to believe. For abundance is to have more than just the minimum necessary.

For argument's sake, let us suppose that poverty, scarcity, or any other form of limitation and lack are good for a child of God, in which case I ask myself: 'Why does Jesus demonstrate abundance, prosperity, and wealth wherever there is a lack?' I, therefore, invite you to ask this question several times a day until you receive your own answer from within, given that there is an omnipresent power that answers all our questions.

Imitate God Himself

God also multiplies: "God blessed them, saying, be fruitful and multiply, and fill the waters in the seas, and let birds multiply on the earth" (*Genesis 1:22*, New American Standard Bible).

God does not content Himself with the little. When He created the heaven and the earth and then saw that the earth was dark and empty, He did not leave it empty. He created the light: "Then God said, 'let there be lights in the expanse of the heavens to separate the day from the night, and let them be for signs and for seasons and for days and years; and let them be for lights in the expanse of the heavens to give light on the earth'; and it was so"(*Genesis 1: 14-15*, Berean Study Bible).

Now, we all know that God and Jesus multiply! Then, why not us?

Exercise

Study the behavior of the ten or hundred richest people in the world and then check to see if they are determined, decisive, and full of faith in themselves and their creative powers. Also, check to see if these people are hesitant and fearful. Do the same exercise with the ten or one hundred world champions in sports. This will give you a good idea of the importance that faith plays in the success of any human endeavor.

By developing your faith and strengthening it, you will easily move your mountains and get results faster. Let us finish this chapter with this Holy Bible verse: "Jesus said unto him, 'if you can believe, all things are possible to him that believes'" (*Mark 9:23*, King James 2000 Bible).

From now on, when you have a challenge in your life, know that you can solve this challenge by faith and actions because everything is possible for you since the powers of creation are in you.

Chapter 6

Analyze and Evaluate Your Results

Control, analysis, and evaluation of physical and mental actions are important in all human activities; they constitute the best method of continuous improvement to help you to achieve outstanding results in all areas of your life.

Assessment Frequency

Regarding the frequency of assessment, several approaches exist. Some people think that you should evaluate yourself once a year. We all recall New Year's resolutions. Others practice self-evaluation every six months. Others still, consistently complete assessments every four, three months, or even every month. I also hear about weekly assessments. I believe we must evaluate every action moment by moment and summarize at the end of the day before going to bed. Why such frequency and diligence? Simply because, in life, many events happen to us during a day. Therefore, waiting several days, weeks, or months before analyzing your actions is too risky if you look to attain success in a reasonable time because you risk forgetting too many details or neglecting to correct errors quickly enough before the next client, transaction, or action.

Let us analyze this example together: You meet a customer. If the relationship progresses well, you congratulate yourself. You thank God or the Universe for this successful outcome. Then you wonder: 'How can I do to do even better next time?' Some people may wonder why we need to ponder further improvement when things are already going very well;

the answer is very simple: We should always endeavor to improve whether things are going well or not, because the capacity of the human being to improve is infinite. There is always the potential for improvement in all areas of our lives.

If things do not go well, we also ask ourselves the same question: 'What can I do even to do better next time?' You must continue to ask this question until your intuition answers your question because we have infinite potential if we rely on the Creator who responds to us through our intuition, as well as signs and other entities within our environment. These entities can be human beings or any other object in your environment. So be alert for any signal of response to your question. Then, implement the response immediately – before the next client, transaction, or action, whenever possible. In some cases, implementing the improvement may take time, but always do it as soon as possible to maximize your chances of success.

When you meet a customer and things go wrong; you do not have to blame yourself or anyone else. Just repeat the following statement until you feel good; it will change your vibration and return it to a vibration of love and gratitude to attract another client and be successful: "God, I love you; thank you for my blessings." You can also keep asking the question 'what is good in this situation?' until you get the answer.

At this point, I hope you understand that the one, who evaluates each transaction or situation and then adjusts his or her aim, will achieve better results and attain success more quickly than the one who waits months or a year to assess one's actions.

We live in a changing and evolving Universe; I have discovered that one of the keys to accepting and adjusting to this change and evolution is to practice systematic and automatic evaluation. The word 'automatic' is important because some people, even before testing this practice, will start by judging it – focusing on all the difficult and seemingly impossible points and finding thousands of excuses for why it will not work. Also, because every attitude or skill that you plant in your subconscious mind becomes automatic in the physical world.

What we need to recognize is that every human being is very intelligent in doing whatever he or she wants to achieve; however, some people use their intelligence to stay in situations that are neither to their advantage nor for their success. The same intelligence they use to stay in the state of mediocrity can be used to succeed.

While ignoring to recognize that, their mental attitude is an attitude of creating difficulties and impossibilities that will surely appear on their way because we harvest what we sow.

Now, some people could say that, 'they do not have time to evaluate themselves after every interaction'. My reply to them is this: "You can certainly have a lot of things to do that could prevent you from evaluating every interaction as it occurs; but, remember that everything that you learn and repeat becomes automatic and easy". Therefore, you can do it, and there is no reason to wait a year before making your assessment if you want to quickly achieve exceptional results.

Example

Let us analyze another example: I worked with a partner on a project to evaluate a certain market before deciding to invest in it. At one point, the partner told me that, 'after a while, we would have to stop to evaluate ourselves and see what needs to be improved.' I was surprised, shocked even. I replied, 'why wait? We should evaluate ourselves on each action.' I do not know if he understood my statement.

Please, note that there are always opportunities for short-term or medium-term adjustments, but this does not override the need to evaluate each action or transaction.

If our goal is to create our wealth in a disciplined and organized way, not haphazardly, we should put everything in place for assured, predictable, and reproducible success. To achieve our goals, it is important to check, evaluate, and monitor our results to see if we are still on track.

Analyzing our results allows us to identify places where we can improve our thinking in order to improve what we manifest in the physical world.

Note that the process always begins inwardly, within our minds – we start by working on our thoughts. Then, we take action to improve our results in the physical world, based on our positive thoughts.

Within our minds, we use our imagination, visualization, and affirmations to create what we want regardless of the 'reality' we see with our five senses in the physical world as well as the emotions associated with what we see around us. Then, we analyze our results as they appear in the physical world around us to measure our success and recognize what we need to improve. We remain disciplined, knowing that we are responsible for our results.

These Bible verses support the ideas above:

- "Do not conform to the pattern of this world, but be transformed by the renewing of your mind. Then you will be able to test and approve what God's will is – his good, pleasing and perfect will" (*Romans 12: 2*, New International Version).

- "You were taught, with regard to your former way of life, to put off your old self, which is being corrupted by its deceitful desires; to be made new in the attitude of your minds" (*Ephesians 4: 22-23*, New International Version).

Chapter 7

Realize the Miracle of Multiplication

If you study[6] carefully the world's biggest fortunes, you will discover that all the people who created these fortunes made them on the basis of multiple sources of income. Most often, the bulk of their wealth comes from one source of income; however, other sources of income are typically involved. Most people focus solely on one main source of wealth and forget that, behind this main source, other income opportunities contribute to their overall fortune. Therefore, the world's biggest fortunes have multiple sources of income. You too can do the same.

Example

For example, these people have first and foremost a main source of income to start; then their money that is not inverted directly into the main source is placed in investment funds, stocks, and other assets that earn them money. Their companies own others companies. Some of these people are counselors to help others getting rich; they have also probably written books to share their knowledge, wisdom, and experience with other individuals wishing to create wealth in their lives. So we see in this simplistic example that wealth develops with multiple sources of income.

Therefore, you should never be satisfied with just one source of income. The world is changing and so are the needs of individuals in it. To be able to face any eventuality and thus limit the risks associated with

6. Forbes, 2018, *THE BILLIONAIRES 2018* [viewed 24 September 2018]. Available from: https://www.forbes.com/billionaires/#567be50c251c

any one investment, the solution is to gradually create multiple sources of income. Wealth creation does not need to stop at a few services or products; it must grow continuously in response to the needs of individuals and their global environment.

Life is constantly expanding; therefore, our wealth must constantly expand. Some people concentrate only in one area of activity, and when a problem arises in that area, they fall into ruin. Your wealth must be created so that it can withstand any eventuality.

Please, do not confuse the gradual creation of multiple sources of income with having multiple jobs because we all have only twenty-four hours in a day. In a job, someone else or another entity controls your ability to progress and your physical presence is usually required. You are limited by your need to be physically present – if you become ill or need to take time away from your job, your income is affected.

On the other hand, in a well-established business, you can infinitely multiply the number of products and services you sell without being physical present. This means that you can be sleeping and your products and services will continue to earn you money and increase your wealth. So there is really a big difference between having a 'job' and building other income streams.

Creating multiple sources of income is not as difficult as you might think; you just have to start with a source of income, master it and then gradually test and add other sources of revenue. You have to be constantly looking for profitable opportunities.

Pay particular attention to the word 'test' because some opportunities can look very promising on paper but, in practice, present many unforeseen issues that must be solved through strategy and intelligence.

It is not necessary for you to manage your multiple sources of income singlehandedly. You can find experienced managers or organizations with demonstrated results that you can trust to help you.

If, for example, you buy a five-hundred-unit residential building and you have no experience in property management, it would be wise to hire a specialized and experienced management company to help you. If you like management, ensure you get the necessary training. To be successful takes preparation, practice, and continuous training.

Generally, you must use your time to do what you really like to do in life, but not have to work. Of course, you have to work to put businesses that will give you financial freedom in place and stabilize them; but as soon as they are in place and stabilized, find ways to use your time to do what you love and have fun.

Some people will tell you to focus on one area of business to create wealth by choosing work that you like or that is associated with your passion. Some of the world's biggest fortunes have started to create their fortune through one particular business. But, quickly, these people then developed additional sources of secondary income. These people did not limit themselves for very long with only one source of income because they know well the risks involved.

In my opinion, doing business in one area is too limiting in relation to the potential that the Creator put in a human being; you are more powerful than you think you are and, you must use this power as much as you can right now.

If you choose to acquire most of your wealth in one area, that is fine. But, know that you can hire the services and knowledge of an individual consultant, or an organization, that does what you want better than you in other areas.

On the website for this book, you will find a list of areas of business opportunities that you can explore, according to your personal interests and strengths, to create additional sources of income.

As I've already advised above, one technique I often use is to look at a community, identify their needs, and see how well I can create a service or product to meet those needs; this technique allows me to be very creative, unlike those who think that all the best ideas for creating wealth have already been used. We must continually apply this technique because the Universe is truly abundant.

In my case, I had to test several business opportunities before finding the ones that best fit my personality and my expectations. In fact, I still continue to test businesses, because this way of accumulating wealth is an endless job – we must never stop or give up. We must continually seek to improve ourselves, our services or products, based on the joy and pleasure of advancing. I will repeat it often so that it becomes a natural habit for you as we are intended to create unlimited wealth.

Chapter 8

Persist! Persist! Persist!

L et's begin by repeating a reflection from the Holy Bible, which instructs us that we must not doubt we must always have faith: "But he must ask in faith, without doubting, because he who doubts is like a wave of the sea, blown and tossed by the wind. That man should not expect to receive anything from the Lord. He is a double-minded man, unstable in all his ways" (*James 1: 6-8*, Berean Study Bible).

One point to remember here is the detrimental effect of hesitation; all successful people are decisive people who do not hesitate. Unsuccessful people are often hesitant and doubtful. But, opportunity responds to speed of reaction and decision. It is well known that nothing can stop a determined human being in the faith; so use this saying to your advantage.

Some inventions have succeeded on the first try; but even they required improvements to create a marketable version. Moreover, the word 'try' indicates that it is neither yet finished nor definitive. We, therefore, observe that all great human achievements require persistence. Think about planes, cars, software, drugs, the Internet, and anything else around you as you read this book – they have all undergone significant development and improvement. This principle also applies to our success and the creation of our wealth.

When we are not aware of the principle of persistence in any human activity, we can become discouraged very quickly by the first hurdle on the road to our success. We allow the fear of failing, and what others will say if we fail, to take over. As a result, we do not produce anything exceptional for ourselves or for others. We limit ourselves to mediocrity and what everyone else does. The truth is that exceptionally successful people do not follow the crowd or average behavior. Successful people lead. And we all have a leader in us, which we can easily develop for our good and the good of others. We must overcome fear and mediocrity by interpreting failure as a positive and strategic element of our success or, even better, a business partner on the path of creating our wealth. Here are some tools to develop persistence and overcome fear:

1. Learn continuously;
2. Continually improve;
3. Always do the best you can in every act and action;
4. Be determined and enthusiastic;
5. Never stop trying, never give up;
6. Verify that your actions and decisions are based on principles of success;
7. Always test and experiment new ideas.

Learn Continuously

We have already addressed learning in other chapters; we approach it again here as a way to overcome hesitation:

Both fear of change and fear of committing to the unknown can cause us to hesitate when starting a business or investing in an opportunity. Strategic and targeted learning and training are the solutions to overcoming hesitation, because self-confidence grows with the acquisition of applied knowledge. As already mentioned above, I identify two forms of learning:

Learning from Others (External)

This form is 'classical learning'. We can receive training from an individual in a formal environment, for example in a classroom or at a seminar or a material support such as book, sound material, audiovisual material, etc. I do not invest in a business without prior training. Today, the opportunities for training and self-training are endless. It is, therefore, a good practice to take advantage of this before investing in a project to maximize our chances of success.

Self-learning (Internal)

It is vitally important to learn from yourself. Self-learning includes many aspects: Physical actions, inner mental conditioning, our thoughts, emotions, customer relationships, and all those involved in daily interactions.

If we pay attention to all these elements constantly for the constructive purpose of improving them, and take good notes as if we must then teach this to another person, we will become an expert in our field.

Improve Yourself Continuously

After each action, whether the result of the action is positive or negative, you always have to ask yourself: 'How can you do better?' Or, 'How can I improve this or that aspect of my job?'

Most people, who want to continuously improve, focus only on what has not worked. I go further, I constantly wonder about the outcome of each action. This attitude will make you more creative and innovative.

Always Do the Best You Can in Every Act and Action

Do everything you do, well, as if you do it for God as the Holy Bible instructs us: "Serve with good will, as to the Lord and not to men, because you know that the Lord will reward each one for whatever good he does, whether he is slave or free" (*Ephesians 6:7-8*, Berean Study Bible).

Whenever I finish a job, I stop and ask myself this question: Did I really give my best to the best of my abilities and my available means? This attitude reduces stress and mitigates doubt or regrets if the desired result is not achieved, because you know that you gave your best effort under the circumstances and open the way to learning from the results to do better next time.

Be Determined and Enthusiastic

When you have decided to start a project, put all your mental and physical resources to work to achieve the project's goal without doubting anything. Make sure, at all times, that your thoughts, emotions, and physical actions are all aimed toward achieving the desired result. Feel the joy of the goal already achieved, and then visualize the many awards of achieving the goal. Undoubtedly, we now know that success begins first in mind, before it materializes in the physical world.

Never Stop Trying, Never Give Up

Never give up – the person who achieves success is simply the person who does not stop and does not give up on his or her way to achieving his or her goals.

Instead of finding a thousand reasons to stop, let us imagine just one or two good reasons for continuing to enrich ourselves. And for why it is possible.

Verify That Your Actions and Decisions Are Based on Principles of Success

Often, people who do not dare to take action to consciously change their lives use a variety of excuses to justify their inaction. I use the word 'consciously' because we are constantly undergoing change unconsciously. Change is a law of nature, which is never static, as some people think or wish. Undeniably, permanent full-time jobs have existed and still exist. There are people who like this type of job which is correct. The point is: In addition to your full-time job create something that you can control and change deliberately because you are creators. Your creative power must be used in all areas for a better life.

If you do not courageously act to consciously create change now in an orderly manner, your environment, nature, or the Universe, will change you without asking your opinion. Therefore, it is in your best interest to create your change consciously to be proud of being the master of your destiny.

One of the most common excuses is lack of money. Remember that we must always start with the means we have and never stop improving. If these people take the time to learn the basics of success and wealth accumulation, they will understand that money is only one element in the process of wealth accumulation and is not necessarily a block to achievement. We all know that people who win the lottery do not necessarily stay rich. The truth is that it takes the consciousness of success, abundance, prosperity, and wealth, to experience lasting success, abundance, prosperity, and wealth in your life.

Always Test and Experiment New Ideas

Warning! When I talk about testing, I'm not saying to just try out of curiosity to see if a deal in a certain market will succeed or not and then find excuses for not continuing.

For me, testing means that, after diligently analyzing the risks, we decide to enter a market in a progressive and disciplined way to discover and learn what we do not already know from the knowledge available on the market in study. With this approach, each test provides an opportunity for learning that will improve the result of the next test. Then, we repeat this process until the desired result is achieved. The key word here is learning.

What is the expected result? After a few tests, followed by reasonable adjustments and assessments, we may reach one of three conclusions:

1. **The market does not match our expectations:** We stop exploring that particular market to explore other options, with the knowledge gained up to that point.

2. **The market corresponds with our expectations:** We continue our experiment to gain first-hand expertise in the market.

3. **This is not the time to invest in this market:** We are interested in this market but determine we should leave it for a later time. We record our experience with notes on the knowledge and expertise we gained from this test, in order to ensure that we do not have to start from scratch when we are ready to invest in this market in the future.

When we embark on a new business, all the seemingly insurmountable problems or difficulties that we face are simply the challenges associated with this specific type of environment. The people who have already succeeded in this environment have lived these challenges and developed techniques to overcome them easily. We can benefit from their experience by using the services of an excellent consultant who can show us convincing results in the environment. We can also practice continuous learning in different forms, such as in a classroom, online, through books, etc.

When pondering persistence, I often consider hundred-meter runners at the Olympic Games. An athlete who stops before the finish line loses automatically. To win, not only must an athlete run faster than all other athletes do, but also, and above all, he or she must not stop before reaching the final line.

This example is not intended to emphasize competition, but rather the idea that we must never stop until we reach our goal. We live in an abundant Universe, so we do not need to win our wealth by competing for it from a pool of limited resources. Resources are abundant and unlimited in a very generous Universe that gives to those who ask, seek, knock, and believe. This is what the Bible teaches us in (*Matthew 7: 7-8*, Berean Study Bible).

Also, consider a child learning to walk. When a child learns to walk, the child often falls but gets up and continues. Sometimes the child falls, laughs, then gets up and keeps running. The child repeats, repeats, and repeats until he or she can walk like everyone else. This example is very striking for me because, as in all human endeavors, we must always keep in mind that there may be moments when we will fall, but in the same spirit, we must always rise back up and continue until we get what we want.

Some people are afraid to start because they fear the challenges or shame when they fall. But I ask them these questions: How many times does a child who is learning to walk fall before he or she can walk correctly? Does the child decide to stop learning to walk because he or she has already fallen several times? Certainly not! The child continues to try until he or she succeeds. As Napoleon Hill[7] so aptly put it: "A quitter never wins and a winner never quits".

As I have already stated: We do not engage in any business without having analyzed it in advance. But, do not let anything stop you, or distract you from your goals because your desire is precious and unique to you. If you do not realize your desire, no one will do it and that will be a loss for all of us because your good desire advances you and others.

Look around at the number of new inventions we use today: Telephone, radio, television, internet, airplane, and many more; all these things started as desires inside the imaginations of other human beings like you and me. If these people had not brought their desires to fruition in spite of the challenges, we would not benefit today from all these marvels.

---

7. Hill, Napoleon (1937). *Think and Grow Rich*. Chicago, Illinois: Combined Registry Company.

Chapter 9

Enjoy Your Results Now

"This is the day, which the LORD has made; let us rejoice and be glad in it" (*Psalm 118: 24*, New American Standard Bible)! It is certain that we must rejoice at every moment of our life, regardless of our circumstances because it is a blessing to be alive here and now and thus to enjoy the benefits of life.

Here are some exercises I practice to express and feel the joy of being here right now:

During the day, whenever possible, stay calm and place your awareness on your breath peacefully for a few minutes. I also use the following statements:

- Oh God, I love you, thank you for your blessings!
- The joy of the Lord is my strength.

Practice these exercises as often as possible, observe how you feel inside, and then share your feelings with those who are ready to enjoy them. I am very clear about those who are ready to take advantage of them because some people are so negative that they respond to every reference to pleasure in life with ridicule.

We all must have short, medium, and long-term goals; however, we must not lose sight of the fact that we do not know when the life we have in this wonderful world will end. Therefore, throughout this practice of honest process of getting rich, we must realize that we really only have now – the past is gone, the future may never come but the present is here with us now. This is why we must not repeatedly put off our enjoyment and pleasure for later – because this 'later' is not under our control.

We must manage our resources so that we can enjoy some of the fruits of our labor today. We have all heard, at one time or another, the story of people who worked very hard while postponing their pleasure for later; and the later never happened. Today are people who do not deserve the results of these people's sweat who are now enjoying and wasting their inheritance. It is known that people who receive an asset without effort often squander it. Above all, do not get confused with the philosophy of honest process of getting rich that one enriches oneself for our good and for the good of others. Selfishness has no place. Of course, there are good heirs who make the fortunes they received grow. This scenario is not to be confused with the biblical concept of passing on a well-managed inheritance to the children of our children by a rich person who is not selfish: "A good man leaveth an inheritance to his children's children: and the wealth of the sinner is laid up for the just" (*Proverbs 13:22*, King James Bible). We have also seen the example of Jesus performing miracles of multiplication for everyone, not just for a select few.

Also, do not be confused by the notion of delayed gratification. Delayed gratification is not eternal deprivation, it is a strategy used to keep our attention and focus on what is important and immediate, by postponing enjoyment for only a few moments, which is quite reasonable in the life of a human being.

For example, during the writing of this book, when I began to observe that the first seven thousand words were becoming laborious, I quickly created a delayed gratification by telling myself that, after every ten thousand words, I would go see a football game. This promise of pleasure created motivation, courage, and enthusiasm, which made the rest of my writing very fluid and easy. A very important point is: Whatever the conditions, always respect your commitment to reward yourself in order to take advantage of the energy of motivation, courage, and enthusiasm that a human being needs to succeed in everything that he or she undertakes. Try using the delayed gratification strategy and observe the result for yourself.

During this honest process of getting rich, you can allocate and manage your assets using multiple bank accounts or other means, according to the model suggested below:

Account type for:

- The needs of each day;
- Enjoyment and pleasure;
- Donations;
- Education;
- Investments;
- Thrift or savings;
- Taxes;
- Intergenerational legacy.

There is no particular order or priority in the list of accounts above. The idea is to use this list to ensure you have something in each of these accounts. The percentage you deposit in each account remains flexible and at your discretion depending on your situation and needs. The idea is to create the habit of managing money steadily and consistently.

Do not wait to be rich to create these accounts. If you wait, you will never become rich. We are in a process of learning; therefore, we must create these accounts now and start creating the habit of managing money. The amount deposited in each account does not matter. It is the regularity and the habit to manage money that matters.

If you wait, telling yourself that you do not have enough money to start creating these different accounts now, what are you saying to the Universe? Of course, you are emitting vibrations of lack and limitation. Then, what do you think the Universe will return to you in response? It will respond with even more gaps and more limitation. No one can escape this universal law.

The Account for the Needs of Each Day

This account contains the funds to meet daily needs like food, clothing, and other immediate and daily needs.

The Account for Enjoyment and Pleasure

This account is intended to satisfy the needs of pleasure and enjoyment – everything that allows you to feel good. For example: Travel, holidays, and anything that makes you feel good. There is no taboo pleasure here; everything is allowed because it is for you and your life. Let your imagination play to find what you want. Every person is different – that is the beauty of life; so, it is up to everyone to choose and determine how he or she wants to use this account. Other people talk about this account as an account to satisfy the child in you, because you have to know that there are several levels in a human being. There is a level that seeks pleasure; if you smother that child in you, that same child may come back to sabotage your success. Everything is a matter of balance in a whole, evolving, and complex human being.

The Account for Donations

Donations are an important dimension of wealth accumulation. This account is intended to reserve money for this purpose. In this case, we are specifically referring to financial gifts as opposed to several other types of gifts that we will describe in more detail in a later chapter. Some people advise donating at least 10% of their income. I suggest a percentage at the discretion of each person, according to his or her current situation and means. We must bear in mind that it is the creation of habits and actions that count in attracting abundance, prosperity, and wealth.

The Account for Education

One of the keys to long-term, stable wealth accumulation is education. This education must be seen in a broad sense, because we can learn from ourselves, from others, and from our environment on an ongoing basis as a way to constantly improve ourselves. This account is therefore intended for expenses associated with a liberal education.

We can use the money from this account to buy books, take training, attend seminars, and have a counselor, a coach, or a mentor, as well as anything that allows us to grow our awareness of success, abundance, prosperity, and wealth.

Education is very important; this is what the Holy Bible says about the importance of knowledge: "My people are destroyed for lack of knowledge. Because you have rejected knowledge, I also will reject you from being my priest. Since you have forgotten the law of your God, I also will forget your children" (Hosea 4: 6, Berean Study Bible).

The Account for Investments

Investment is a crucial pillar in creating big wealth. One of the activities of a wealth creator is the constant pursuit of opportunity; therefore, this account, allows you to act quickly when the opportunity arises, if after thorough analysis, reasonable, and due diligent verification of all known risks, you decide to commit yourself to it.

The Account for Savings

For short, medium and long-term projects or goals as well as unforeseen events, you can use your savings account. This account can be managed by yourself or in combination with an organization, depending on your level of comfort and investment knowledge.

The Account for Taxes

It is not wise to wait for the tax deadline to check if you have money to pay these taxes. It is strongly advised to save money in this account to pay taxes. You can just deposit the minimum possible that you can afford now and eventually add money, if the money in this account is not enough to pay the taxes when the time comes.

The Account for Intergenerational Legacy

Contrary to what some people think, the process of wealth creation is not a selfish enterprise. Through it, we seek to enrich others as well as ourselves; therefore, it is noble and wise to create an account dedicated to our descendants. This account can also be jointly managed. The Holy Bible approaches it in the same way in this verse: "A good man leaveth an inheritance to his children's children: and the wealth of the sinner is laid up for the just" (*Proverbs 13:22*, King James Bible).

Note that some accounts must be managed by professional organizations with a proven track record. Other accounts can be managed by you. In some cases, accounts can be managed jointly by both you and an organization, depending on your experience and knowledge of strategic investments. Let us recall, once again, that we take every precaution to succeed because we do not succeed by chance; we obtain it by constantly, consciously, and persistently practicing the principles of success. Many people ignore or neglect to act with the required discipline, or simply do not apply it until disaster strikes.

The use of the content of each of these accounts must be disciplined and exclusively dedicated to its defined purpose. However, as a wealth creator, you may encounter investment opportunities in which you will have the choice to borrow from a bank, an organization, or individuals. Eventually, you can also evaluate the possibility of borrowing from your accounts. In this last option, be sure to repay the borrowed funds at the right time; it requires very rigorous discipline because discipline and self-control are among the best qualities of great investors and successful people. Naturally, you will be able to develop all these qualities if you apply the techniques exposed in this book strictly and constantly.

Sometimes when we borrow money from our accounts, we tend to be careless in repayment; it's an attitude to avoid if we want to be successful in the long run.

The expression "creator of wealth" may seem strange to some people, which I understand perfectly. However, in reality, this process is really a system in which we grow forever, because we are in a constantly moving Universe. This honest process of getting rich is not just something like a diploma that we get and then stop, it is about unlimited wealth creation; therefore, it has no end.

It is true that, in this world, most of what we do or learn – for example, like going to school or doing something else – requires entering into a process and, at the end of that process, we get what we call a diploma, and after that, we stop, either to look for a job or to go on to another level. In this process of wealth creation, learning never stops because we live in a dynamic Universe. The human being that we are as an element of the Universe is also constantly growing.

Some people think that, when they stop proactively learning and growing, they are the same person. In reality, this is not true. It is certain that the first day that a person stops doing something, he or she will not realize the negative change even though he or she is falling below his or her skills; however, a few years later, the person will realize it.

Take the example of learning a language: You are learning the language; you master it and speak it correctly and fluently. Then, for some reason, you live in an environment where you no longer use that language; here also, on the first day, you will not notice any difference in your skills in this language. However, after a few years, you will realize that you no longer have the same level of expression in that language.

It is this way for all initiatives that any person undertakes. That is why, in this enrichment process, we are constantly working on ourselves to improve constantly – to improve our services, our products, our strategies, our attitude, our way of thinking – to be constantly a new person for ourselves and for others. We do all this in a spirit of joy, because as stated in the Holy Bible, "A day must be a day of joy and happiness": "This is the day, which the LORD has made; let us rejoice and be glad in it" (*Psalm 118:24*, New American Standard Bible).

People often approach me saying that they have stopped this or that because they have it under control or for some other reason. I smile when I respond, saying that we 'never stop'. We are constantly improving ourselves to be the best we can, in all areas of our lives. Do not confuse this concept with stopping a bad habit – that is actually a self-improvement.

In the same vein, when I meet children, I often tell them that you do not just use your intelligence when you're in a classroom or writing an exam; we must constantly use our intelligence as a habit, in our way of doing things, and in all the circumstances of our lives.

Chapter 10

Give and Help Others

The best way to get rich is to give – to donate! This point is very difficult for most people to understand. Yet, when we know that, everything in the Universe is energy and vibration. Then, we understand that, if a person has great confidence in himself or herself – to the point of emitting the vibration that he or she already has abundance and more than enough – then, he or she is in a position to give, regardless of his or her current financial state. And, the Universe responds by giving back to him or to her what he or she has, in abundance, according to the Law of Cause and Effect.

There are people who say that they do not currently have enough to give to others. They think, 'I will give when I have enough', That is not the right approach. The rule says this: Give what you have, what you can, and never stop giving. The Holy Bible says: "A generous person will prosper; whoever refreshes others will be refreshed" (*Proverbs 11:25*, New International Version}.

The donation does not have to be financial. You can give your time, skills, knowledge, and everything else you can do to serve a community, an organization, or anyone else, in a spirit of joy and pleasure. The key word is "SERVING" generously, without any expectation of getting something in return.

Where to Give Your Donation?

Where to give your donation is a question that comes up often; the answer is very simple though individual to each person; however, it is strongly advised to give to 'productive organizations'. Let me explain what I call a 'productive organization'. If an organization helps individuals to stay in the state they are in, I do not see this organization as 'productive'.

I know a lot of unproductive organizations that help people to perpetually remain in poverty. But, productive organizations are those that help people to find a trade or a job – as some churches do, for instance. When a person leaves a productive organization, he or she becomes better than when he or she is entered. That means that productive organizations help people to move on to better ways of life, rather than keeping them stuck within a particular program or institution.

On any given day, you can donate to someone who has helped you to move forward, who inspired you, and so on. The list is not exhaustive; you can support any tool or system that has inspired you to advance. For example, give to the author of a film, a book, an audio version; to anyone who has somehow helped you to be a better person than you were before you experienced what they offered.

Personally, since I discovered this secret, I always give. For example, when a person brings me a new client with whom I make a deal, I give the person who introduced us something as a thank you. I sometimes find myself in situations where people refuse donations for personal or religious reasons. They say, "I did not make this gesture for the money; it is God who will thank me." I reply that, "God is inside me and will thank you more than my thank you. I know you did not ask for anything". For me, anyone involved in my success gets the fruit of success – this is part of my motto. I always give to people who inspire me, including children. During an event or celebration, if children inspire me, I give them money.

The Vibration of the Donation

Another amazing thing about contributing is that, when you give something, both you and the person who receives it feel a shift internally – a positive vibration – a deep feeling of joy and the pleasure of giving. Where do you think this feeling of joy or well-being is spread? It spreads throughout the Universe and, then, what happens? It returns to us multiplied. It is simply the Law of Cause and Effect always in action. The Holy Bible says: "For as the rain and the snow come down from heaven, And do not return there without watering the earth And making it bear and sprout, And furnishing seed to the sower and bread to the eater; so will My word be which goes forth from My mouth; It will not return to Me empty, Without accomplishing what I desire, And without succeeding in the matter for which I sent it. (*Isaiah 55:10-12*, New American Standard Bible). The simple gesture of giving has indescribable positive ramifications.

If you never donate, you will never experience that feeling – that dimension of life – and, even worse, you will emit limiting vibrations into the Universe. What do you get in return for limitation? Still more limitation – and all when we have evidence that the Universe is abundant.

Some Strange Situations Concerning Donations and Help

We have seen in the preceding section that the act of giving results in at least three kind of vibration: One into the Universe the second as a feeling inside the giver and another one as a feeling inside the receiver. In this section, we present another kind of vibration related to the act of giving when the receiver refuses the gift.

I present here some situations that I find unusual in the act of giving:

One day, in downtown Montreal, I met a man begging on the street; I had approached him nicely to offer him food. He shouted at me, telling me he did not want food but wanted money.

Another time in the subway in Paris, my little sister, Helene, gave money to a beggar; the latter calculated the money received and shouted at my sister that it was not enough.

I was raised and educated in an environment in which we learned to receive with pleasure and humbly say thank you for any gift. As a result, I find it difficult to understand the reaction of some people when they receive. Especially when they receive something that they did not ask for and that the person giving was not obliged to give.

You Receive When You Give or Help Others

We have just seen that when we give something to other people, we receive in return. We receive positive vibration if accepted or negative vibration when rejected, but the Universe will always reward us positively. Therefore, we must always serve with good will. Here is what the Holy Bible says: "Serve with good will, as to the Lord and not to men, because you know that the Lord will reward each one for whatever good he does, whether he is slave or free" (*Ephesians 6:7-8*, Berean Study Bible).

Let us look at an example of positive vibration in the case of training or education.

People who give training often have this experience: You have a good command of your subject; however, every time you give training to a person or people, depending on their questions, you reinforce and readjust your own knowledge of the subject and improve your teaching strategies. You receive also positive feedback in return that helps you to improve your teaching skills.

This often happens to me because I had the privilege of giving a lot of training. I greatly appreciate the feeling that often comes back to me at the end of a training session, making me feel enriched.

For example, if you apply the principles from this book diligently, persistently, and consistently, then expect the level of wealth you want. You can spread the good news of how you achieved it to people around you. You will be surprised when, sometime later, these people meet you and thank you for the book you recommended to them. They tell you that the book really helped them reach their goals; at that moment, you will feel a sense of satisfaction.

I often make suggestions to people who are in difficult situations. Then, they apply the strategies I recommend and I sometimes forgot the help I gave them. A few years later, when these people meet me, they are so happy to tell me the wonderful results that they experienced when they followed my advice, and hearing their feedback always gives me pleasure.

Chapter 11

Cultivate Gratitude, and Always Think Positively

You must constantly cultivate gratitude in all circumstances.

I think life is a gift; therefore, we must continually say thank you to the Universe or to God according to your level of comfort with those words. I presume that any reader who is comfortable with the Holy Bible references will be comfortable with the word "God". I think we are not here by chance. I note here that speed has an influence in the creation of human life; similarly, successful people make their decisions quickly and stick with their decisions without faltering until they achieve their desired results.

Here is one of the statements I often use to express my gratitude to the Universe. Whatever the circumstances, good or bad, I always say:

• God, I love you, thank you for my blessings.

This omnipresent, omniscient, and omnipotent power in which we live, and that also lives within us, is sensitive to the vibration of gratitude.

"The man, who can sincerely thank God for the things which as yet he owns only in imagination, has real faith. He will get rich; he will cause the creation of whatsoever he wants" (*Wallace D. Wattles*).

Let's go back to what the Holy Bible says about gratitude; it teaches us that we must pray constantly and say thank you in all circumstances: "Rejoice always, pray without ceasing, in everything give thanks; for this is the will of God in Christ Jesus for you" (*1 Thessalonians 5: 16-18*, New American Standard Bible).

A Strategy for Changing Energy or Vibration

Indeed, the expression of gratitude can be used as a strategy for changing energy or vibration.

Pay particular attention to the fact that this practice of expressing gratitude is not just a good attitude to develop for the pleasure of doing it or to say that we are applying it, it's deeper than that. There is a profound psychological benefit to the person who expresses it in terms of energy or vibration change. This positive change can be very beneficial in a critical or conflicting situation.

Imagine yourself in a situation in which an event occurs that you perceive as negative. If you stay and persist in this negative perspective, then you emit negative vibrations into the Universe. What will you receive as a response from the Universe? You will logically receive more negative vibrations to match your state of negativity.

You can likely find examples of how negative vibrations bring more negativity in your own experience. Something happens to you, you judge it as negative, you persist in thinking negatively about it and the next series of events are negative also. Hence, we need to learn to control these vibrations and consciously change them. Pay close attention to the word 'conscious' since mastery or perfection does not happen by chance – it happens through the conscious and consistent control of thoughts, emotions, and actions.

Now, consider another example in which a negative event occurs: You remember gratitude and then consciously begin to repeat words or affirmations of love, joy, and gratitude. What signal do you emit into the Universe? Of course, love vibrations! The vibration of love is one of the highest positive vibrations in existence. In response, the Universe sends you even more love back and you automatically feel a deeply positive feeling inside. You have just successfully raised your vibration and continue your day peacefully doing what you have planned – without suffering any negative repercussions due to the negative event. Here is what the Holy Bible says regarding the power of good words or affirmations to control anxiety: "Anxiety weighs down the heart of a man, but a good word cheers it up" (*Proverbs 12:25*, Berean Study Bible).

Constantly and consciously seeking to be in a state of positive vibration also benefits your health since, among other things, when you do not let events control your emotions, you prevent unnecessary stress.

Controlling your vibration also empowers you to control situations with a clear mind so you can make informed and wise strategic decisions about events and quickly regain control of the situation. Demonstrating your power of choice and decision is very useful in the conduct of business.

Exercise

When a negative event occurs, quickly focus consciously on the image of your future goals as if they were already realized and recite affirmations of joy and pleasure continuously for about fifteen to thirty minutes. Then, note how your body feels – you will become aware of the benefits of raising your vibration.

Sometimes, the negative vibration disappears but then reappears a moment later. When that happens, repeat the exercise again. If you continue in this process, your mind may return to thinking about the event, but you will not feel the same level of intensity of negative vibration. You have mastered the control of your emotion in the context of the event, and you can move forward peacefully.

In the conduct of daily business, many 'good', planned events take place; however, unpredictable, 'bad' events can also occur. If you do not have the tools to control your emotions, you can end your day emotionally exhausted and, in the long run, ruin your business. Negative emotions, continued long-term can even negatively affect your health. Hence, the importance of controlling your emotions under all circumstances.

To this end, proactively prepare affirmations of love, gratitude, and joy in advance to avoid having to improvise when you find yourself in a difficult situation. Always be one step ahead of the events in your life.

A person who is aware of his or her internal powers need never suffer, whatever happens. He or she must deliberately develop techniques and methods to be ready for any eventuality. This is possible and this book contains many techniques and methods to help you get there. It's the best approach to creating your destiny and a better life.

Feel the Vibration of Gratitude

To fully understand the vibration of gratitude, remember how you feel when you give something to someone or do a service to someone and the person is satisfied and sincerely thanks you. At that moment, you feel a deep sense of joy, a vibration that makes you want to do even better or even more for the person. As we are created in the image of the power of the Divine Creator or God, and therefore He feels the vibration of gratitude just like us, but in a larger dimension at the height of His powers, and in response, He gives us even more of what we want.

We must therefore constantly send vibrations of gratitude to this supreme power. Likewise, when He receives our vibrations of gratitude, the Universe gives us even more. It is always the principle of Cause and Effect between you and the Universe; your vibration into the Universe comes back to you, usually multiplied.

You can also observe and note that, when you give your all to satisfy a person, and think that, if you were in the place of the person, you would express deep gratitude, but that person does not express any sign of gratitude to you in this context you may feel a sense of frustration. Even if your intention was not to receive something in return, but only just to help a person who needs a service or a help in a neutral way and without ulterior motives.

As the muscles of the body need training and exercise to be developed, Gratitude must also be developed to the point that it is spontaneous, in both our life and our attitude toward our surroundings, others, the Universe, and ourselves.

An exercise to develop gratitude is just to express gratitude to oneself. During a day, you will gradually discover that there are many opportunities to express gratitude to yourself. For example, when driving a car, if a person makes a false move and you still manage to avoid the accident, you congratulate yourself and say 'thank you' to yourself or simply say 'thank you' to the Universe. Each time that a similar situation happens to me, I repeat to myself several times as long as I can, "Thank you, Rémi! You are really an excellent driver; thank God and glory to you".

In this context, I do not care about the person who created the incident; I focus on managing my emotions to continue serenely through my day. Because I realize that, whatever a person focuses on grows. So, I refuse to pay attention to a situation that is not favorable to avoid inflating it – so I do not create more obstacles on my way to my goals and the best life that I am able to create for myself. You will soon see that you can spontaneously say 'thank you' to any gesture that people make to you or to others.

On the other hand, let us remember that gratitude is not expressed only after having received a service or an object of some kind. Gratitude to the Universe or God is an ongoing, continuous action; for example, every morning when I get up and every night before sleeping I identify two or three things in my life for which I decide to express gratitude. This exercise creates a form of connection with something greater than myself, in which I bathe. It is a very grand and pleasant state.

In summary, let us remember that it is not only for good things, good situations, good environments, or events that happen in our life that we must have gratitude, but also for things that appear seemingly negative.

Use the Vibration of Gratitude to Energize Your Visualization Sessions

I just explained that you can express gratitude when you have achieved something, received excellent service, or for your existing assets. However, in reality, gratitude is not limited to those types of things alone. Over the years, I have developed an attitude of gratitude that gives me truly exceptional and, in some cases, extraordinary results. I invite you to practice this technique regularly then judge for yourself.

You can indeed use the vibration of gratitude to amplify your affirmation or visualization sessions; here is an example: Take, two-to-five-minutes to express deep gratitude to the Universe. Then, when the vibration fills you, begin your affirmations or visualizations. You can even repeat the affirmations while visualizing. By the way, as I already mentioned, visualization combined with affirmations gives the best, as well as the fastest, results.

Remember that the Universe loves us so much and, as we are in the Universe and the Universe is in us, nothing can happen to us that is not for our good. At the moment these events occur, we are not aware of their benefits, but sometimes it is later that we realize that an event happened to us to help us to reach a higher level of awareness.

You will realize very quickly that you can change your vibrational state as you desire with respect to any event – whatever the situation or the environment in which you find yourself. This technique also allows you to be in control of your emotions and yourself in difficult and unforeseen situations; you will not experience the situations or emotions of others, but you will decide what emotion to choose or feel.

By doing so, you attract all the good things you want in all areas of your life because we live in a magnetic field. Here is the method to quickly manifest everything you want:

- Find a quiet place;
- Close your eyes;
- Relax physically and mentally;
- Turn your head slightly upwards;
- Be still;
- Count backward from ten to one, or twenty to one, while relaxing more with each breath;
- Ponder, for about one-to-two minutes, something in your life for which you are grateful;
- When you begin to feel the vibration of gratitude; begin your visualization combined with your affirmations;
- At the end of your session, which should last at least fifteen minutes, thank the Universe with gratitude as if you have already received the desire you have visualized.

During your day, have in your mind the image of the desire that you have visualized and accompany it with silent or faint assertions (just enough to hear your own voice) whenever possible.

When you receive the intuition of an action to achieve the desire you have visualized, act quickly without delay, with the means you have right now, and never stop improving.

Apply this technique regularly and you will see your life gradually changing.

I feel a deep sense of gratitude when I contemplate how my father and mother worked hard and smart to help their children find their place in this world.

We have gained this life through our parents, just for that, they deserve our gratitude.

I think that a human being must always propagate deliberate love to emit positive vibrations as often as possible and thus attract positive and beneficial effects back. This attitude does not happen inadvertently; it takes a conscious and consistent behavior at all times.

Always Think Positively

I think you will agree with me when I say that the power of positive thinking is astonishing.

The concept that your mind can change your entire life for the better seems too good to be true. However, I can tell you that I have truly experienced and witnessed the advantage of focusing and thinking about the positive side of any event and what it brings. Positive thinking brings a positive attitude and actions, which lead to outstanding results.

Have you ever wonder what successful people think about all day long? The answer is very simple: They always think about what they want and how to get it, thereby developing a positive attitude that attracts what they want. This mental attitude actually changes your life.

A positive thinker anticipates success, abundance, prosperity, and wealth and believes in overcoming any obstacle and difficulty on his or her way to success. Belief is the key word here – because, to gain full use of it in your life, you need to be more than just aware of its existence, you have to adopt the attitude of positive thinking in everything you do. You will feel happier and in control of your life when you think of what you want and how to get it in faith.

Let us now explore together some important aspects of adopting the attitude of always thinking positively in all the circumstances of our lives:

- The power of positive thinking;
- Practicing positive thinking;
- Using positive thinking to develop your intuition;
- Using positive thinking to discover your purpose;
- How to apply positive thinking;
- Improving your life with positive thinking;
- Attracting more abundance with positive thinking;
- Attracting more money with positive thinking;
- Facing challenging times with positive thinking;

The Power of Positive Thinking

The fact is that your thoughts define your actions; your actions produce your results. There is a creative power in thinking. Successful people always seek the lesson and value in any setback. Instead of getting upset and blaming someone else for what has happened, they take control over their emotions by saying "what can I learn from this experience?" or "what is good in this experience?" It is what Napoleon Hill[8] calls to "Learn from adversity and defeat". The power of positive thinking is revealed in the daily practice of positive thinking.

The mind learns through repetition of thoughts; therefore, daily repetition is the key to experience the real power of positive thinking as it comes from it. In order to reap the rewards of the power of positive thinking, you need to keep practicing and applying positive thinking every day and in every circumstance. This means that you have to change the way you see and perceive things, change your words, actions, and persistently control and change what you think. The power of positive thinking requires that you eliminate negative thinking and this has to be done on a daily basis.

Every day, we have thousands and thousands of thoughts. Most of them are meaningless and will have little or no impact on us. However, within all these thoughts are a number of negative thoughts and these are the thoughts that will work against you and prohibit you from succeeding. You have to control and change those negative thoughts that are tied to negative beliefs and attitudes. If you repeatedly say something negative, or use a negative phrase, you likely have a negative belief tied to that negative thought. Hence, substitute those negative thoughts, which are tied to negative or limiting beliefs, immediately. The best way to do that is to replace them with positive thoughts and you have to do this regularly using affirmations and visualizations.

You will be able to do this if you are paying attention to what you are thinking and saying. Nevertheless, as time goes on, you will likely forget because the mind will go back to what it knows and will call upon those negative thoughts again. That is why you need to pay attention to those negative thoughts as often as possible and replace them with positive affirmations and visualizations.

The true power of positive thinking comes when you apply positive thinking automatically. That happens when you automatically have positive thoughts, when you no longer repeat negative statements, and when your mind is filled with more positive thoughts than negative thoughts.

---

8. Hill, Napoleon (1994). *Napoleon Hill's Keys to Success: The 17 Principles of Personal Achievement*, Dutton Adult

When you have positive thinking in place, you begin to attract positive situations and people, and you begin to take positive action so that you enjoy a more successful, happier and rewarding life.

Individuals who apply positive thinking systematically are naturally more optimistic and upbeat. They enjoy life and they bounce back from setbacks more quickly than negative thinkers do. It seems like negative thinkers love setbacks. It is not easy for a chronic negative thinker to apply positive thinking.

If that statement applies in your case, you will find it hard to believe that things could be positive. You will have some setbacks and you will want to continue thinking negative thoughts because that is what your mind knows and is accustomed to. To change this, you need to diligently change your negative thinking to positive.

Consequently, every moment, monitor your thinking. That attitude is the starting point of self-mastery. Track your thoughts. Change the negative thoughts to positive thoughts as soon as possible. Keep on doing this daily until you get result. The more often you do this exercise, the sooner your mind will move from being negative most of the time to being positive. This is the path to begin to develop and use the power of positive thinking to get greater success in your life.

Practicing Positive Thinking

As already stated, positive thinking makes a huge difference; when you have a positive mindset and constantly think positively you are more confident and you attract positive people into your life.

However, in order to get the most out of positive thinking you need to practice it every day. This can be challenging especially for a chronically negative person – the kind that always looks at what is wrong and what might go wrong in every project before starting it.

To help you practice positive thinking, here are some suggestions that you can apply; you have to follow these suggestions daily in order to create a pattern of positive thinking that will lead to success and more happiness:

- Systematically and deliberately cultivate a positive mental attitude;

- Always think of how things might work out for you in a good way. Think about why you can easily achieve your goals instead of why you cannot. Find many reasons why you can succeed and push your mind to think of how great things would be once you succeed. See the end result in your imagination;

- In every situation, look for winning alternatives. Be open to any possibility. Be willing to explore all options and be willing to learn something new and take a positive attitude in all situations. Do not look only for the worst side of a situation but rather thinking about the best and explore other positive solutions;

- Cultivate confidence by thinking of the best possible outcome in situations. This is important because, when you regularly think of the best possible outcome, you are making major strides in developing positive thinking and you start to form a healthy and positive attitude;

- The Universe is generous; therefore, be grateful in every situation. Appreciate often the good and positive things in your life. Positive thinkers appreciate what they have and appreciate even the small but good things in their life. It can be anything like a warm meal, a pleasant conversation with a friend or colleague, or something as big as getting a promotion. Be grateful for all the wonderful things in your life to get more;

- We are responsible for what happens in our life. Therefore, when we do something that does not empower us to succeed or does not live up to our expectations, we should learn from it and move forward. Always, focus on the positive aspects of what happened but learn from your tribulations;

- Consciously take control of your thoughts and avoid dwelling on negative thoughts as much as possible. You could have some negative thoughts; nevertheless, the negative thoughts that do not allow you to succeed must be replaced immediately by positive thoughts. Track your thoughts and get rid of the negative thoughts as soon as possible. Replace them with positive thoughts and you will develop positive beliefs that advance you;

- Have confidence in yourself. You can achieve anything you want. Have faith that you can and you will. Be positive and optimistic about your life and you will enjoy more success.

Use these simple suggestions daily and you will start developing a habit of practicing positive thinking. Once that habit takes hold, your subconscious mind responds by creating more and more positive situations. You will not see changes overnight. It will take some time. However, you will begin to see small changes quickly.

You may begin to attract new friends and circumstances; you may get new opportunities – consequently, pay attention. The changes are taking place in the background. Remember, positive thinking always leads to a better, more rewarding and successful life. Negative thinking only leads to more misery. Keep your mind positive, keep your thoughts positive, and enjoy life – it is possible for you.

Using Positive Thinking to Develop your Intuition

It is easy to develop your intuition using positive thinking in order to enjoy better results. By applying positive thinking, you will be able to better understand and recognize your intuitive voice and message because there is no obstruction in your mind caused by negative thoughts.

Your intuition is always speaking, always communicating and always working for you. Unfortunately, negative thoughts could prevent you from receiving those messages. The message from your intuition is positive, it only wants to help you, guide you, and make your life better. On the other hand, when you do not have a positive mindset, when your mind is negative and filled with clutter, you will not be able to recognize or understand your intuition. Therefore, you will not be able to work with it consequently; thus, you lose an important partner in your success.

When you apply positive thinking, you are able to get rid of that clutter, eliminate the negative thinking, and recognize your intuition easily when it communicates.

The best way to develop your intuition is to think about what guidance you want. You should think positively about the guidance you want and that means keeping the request or question in the positive tense. Then, trust that you will get the answer and this is where positive thinking comes into play. You see, your intuition is always at work, and you can develop your intuition when you trust that you will get the answer you want from it.

However, many years of negative thinking can prevent you from recognizing and trusting your intuition, because you will not pay attention to it. You will not be able to understand the intuitive guidance if you have too much negative thinking. Negative thinking leads to doubt, it forces you to question your intuition, not trust it and, in the end, you could do the opposite of what your intuition tells you and that gets you in more trouble because your are doubtful and hesitant.

Through positive thinking, you recognize your intuition and trust it so that you will get your answer, and you trust that your intuition will give you the right answer and guidance that is best for you. In other words, *you trust life.*

Surely, this is the way positive thinking helps you develop your intuition to eliminate the clutter and remove the doubt that prevents you from getting the results that you deserve. Positive thinking empowers you to develop your intuition in a way that helps you to recognize it so that you can communicate easily with it for a better life.

Using Positive Thinking to Discover Your Purpose

You should know your purpose in life. If you have a purpose and you follow your passion, you live a life with purpose, you enjoy your life, you achieve success and you wake up in the mornings excited because you are going to achieve your worthy ideal.[9]

Most people do not live this way; they do not follow their calling and do not enjoy life the way they should. Most people will say that they do not know what they want to do. Then, when you give them suggestions, they will give you a long list of reasons and excuses why they cannot do what they want to do or what you suggest. Their mind is so filled with negative thoughts that create negative thinking patterns, which have become part of who they are, what they do, what they have, and the results that they get in their life.

In order to discover your calling and enjoy life, you have to believe that you can do what you want and, to develop that kind of belief, you need to have a positive thinking pattern in place. To do so, your mind should be filled with positive thoughts most of the time. Those positive thoughts could guide you toward discovering your purpose in life.

When you begin to play the game of replacing your negative thoughts with positive thoughts, you naturally begin to believe in yourself. Then when you start to think about your calling or doing what you enjoy; you are able to discover that calling more easily because you will believe that

---

9. Earl Nightingale (1957), *The Strangest Secret audio program.* Nightingale-Conant

you can. This is how positive thinking supports you and allows you to follow your calling or your passion. Any doubt or negative thoughts will impede your ability to discover your calling, so think positively about your ideal life. Think about what you like doing. Then start doing it right now without delay.

When you notice some negative thoughts creeping in, saying you cannot do what you like, or what you want, then remove those thoughts by replacing them with positive thoughts of courage and enthusiasm. As you do this more and more, you will begin to discover your calling, your purpose, and you will be creating a positive thinking pattern that will support your passion and enable you to enjoy success.

How to Apply Positive Thinking

Applying positive thinking could seem difficult for some people. In fact, it is very easy because it is like playing a game with your own thoughts. Positive thinking is something that should be done in advance before things go wrong. Unfortunately, most people begin using positive thinking when it is too late. They only start trying to apply positive thinking *after* something bad has happened, or something has gone wrong. Trying to apply positive thinking at that time is like pouring a bucket of water on a raging fire. The flames are spreading very quickly and you need to take drastic measures. In that context, it is too late so you have to make conscious efforts to proactively overcome negative thoughts.

Indeed, positive thinking works better when you apply it before things go wrong. Nevertheless, let us say you are at the point where things have gone wrong and now you want to apply positive thinking. How do you make it work?

One approach to making positive thinking work once things have gone wrong is to change the way you see things, shifting your thoughts to the positive – and that means getting rid of the negative thoughts that continually come up. Your mind will want to think about what went wrong and continually analyze the situation, hoping to find a solution, or maybe you think you can go back and fix things so that they will be what they once were. This is the mind playing tricks on you, it just wants you to stay where you are, analyze the situation repeatedly, and try to go back to the way things were. When that happens, you need to push the mind forward and start thinking about what you want to happen next.

You can also take three deep breaths, while concentrating on one of your hobbies or something that makes you laugh. Keep asking yourself 'what is good in this situation?' until you get a positive answer.

You should think of all the positive things you could learn from what went wrong so that you learn from past mistakes and then start filling your mind with positive thoughts that focus on how you can be successful next time. This attitude will take practice; therefore, you have to repeatedly push your mind to think positively, to learn from past mistakes, and to focus on what you want next. You cannot do this occasionally or once a day. It is a constant exercise that you have to work at, and that means *every day* throughout the day. Meanwhile, your mind will want to focus on the negative, as it has been accustomed to doing. If you're not used to thinking positively, or if you are not normally, a positive person then it may take even longer to move past the setback or create the changes you want.

Once you are regularly positive, then your mind is used to being positive, upbeat, and optimistic, and it is easier for you to bounce back from setbacks when things go wrong. That is because your mind is familiar to being positive and you have a belief that things will get better. So, instead of waiting for something to go wrong to try to apply positive thinking, start being more positive and optimistic today.

I present here a few practical things that you can do to help you apply positive thinking and to become more positive:

- Decide to believe, that it is possible for you to be a positive thinker;
- Every day, think of at least five things that you enjoyed by focusing on positive details only. This can be anything, even a nice cup of coffee, spending time with a friend, or enjoying a great meal. Just pick any five things and focus on them daily;
- Do random acts of kindness that lead to a positive outcome at least three times a day. For example, holding a door open for someone without any expectation, or helping somebody – anything that is positive and makes somebody else feel good;
- At night, before going to bed, think of at least five things that you did well during the day and acknowledge your positive qualities;
- Choose to say at least five positive things to somebody during the day; because what we do to others comes back to us greatly multiplied;

- Acknowledge that you can get everything you want from this life; therefore, do not complain – be positive!

Take the time to write those suggestions and memorize them so that they will be easy to use, because the more often you use these suggestions, the sooner you will become more positive and confident.

Keep in mind that you have to *practice* being positive and that means doing things differently while eliminating all the negative thoughts. So, start right now to apply positive thinking in every area of your life by keeping track of your thoughts and your progress. Once you become more and more positive and confident you will begin to see positive coincidences unfold in your life – that is when things will start to work out more often for you.

Improving your Life with Positive Thinking

To improve your life, apply positive thinking regularly, to create dramatic and long-lasting changes. Yet, you have to apply positive thinking *correctly* and, in this book, I will outline a few simple steps you can follow and work with.

There is no quick solution to developing positive thinking to improve your life. Positive thinking is something that you have to work with and implement over a period of time. That means that any changes you want to make will also take some time, depending on your situation and personality. There is no quick fix and, just because you start applying positive thinking today, does not mean that your life will change tomorrow. However, it *will change* in long run. It takes time for new positive thinking patterns to take hold. Nevertheless, there is a real power in positive thinking – you just need some patience to see it pay off. Most of us are not taught to think positively and no one ever really tells you how to develop positive thinking. Instead, you likely have more negative thoughts than positive. In a given situation, you likely think negatively before having positive thoughts. If that is the case, you will end up creating more and more negative situations.

As time goes on, and things do not work out or go the way you want, you realize that you need to change things in your life – mainly because you are not getting what you want from life. You are not getting what you want because your mind is filled with negative thoughts and doubts. Your subconscious simply creates what you regularly think about and believe. Consequently, if you are filled with negative thoughts, then you likely have more of what you do not want in life. Things cannot always work out the way you want, if you are constantly negative.

Someone may suggest that you practice positive thinking and everything will change. Of course, that is easier said than done. Hence, how do you create changes by working with positive thinking?

Create and work with positive affirmations, but, and this is important, make sure your positive affirmations are focused on what you want. They should be positive and they should address or reflect the changes you want – the end result or the solution. This is another important step in applying positive thinking to create changes. Let us say that you decide to apply positive thinking: Think about what you want to change or improve in your life; you may want to:

- Make more money. Make that a goal and decide how much you want to make. Do not be vague;

- Meet the right life partner and have a terrific relationship. Start thinking about the dynamics of this new relationship and what kind of person you want to be with;

- Change your job. Think about the kind of job you want and where you want it.

As soon as you know what you want, think about the positive things that you can do to achieve that goal. Then, start doing them as soon as possible. Do not delay.

Once you begin to have doubts, get rid of them by replacing those thoughts of doubt with positive thoughts that focus on what you want to achieve. Think of why you *can* achieve what you want, not why you cannot. This kind of positive thinking gets your mind focused on why you can achieve your goals, provides you with positive feedback so that you encourage yourself to go forward, and gives you a clear direction or a clear path to follow.

To summarize, here is what you can do to apply positive thinking to create changes in your life and how positive thinking can play an important role in the process. Be patient because, when you apply positive thinking, your mind will take some time to adjust and accept your new thoughts. Your subconscious mind will also take some time to adjust. Change will happen but do not expect it to happen overnight. Continue to think about what you want. Stop thinking about what is wrong and what you do not want. Only focus on what you want, positively:

- Create strong positive affirmations that you can recite regularly to occupy your mind with what you want;
- Decide what you want and be clear about it.
- Perform actions to do things that can help you achieve your goals and create the changes you want;
- Eliminate thoughts of doubt and uncertainty;
- Motivate and encourage yourself positively by reading books like this one.

Attracting More Abundance with Positive Thinking

As the Universe is abundant, therefore, we should live in abundance in every way. Before you can commence to attract abundance, you have to decide what abundance means to you; otherwise, you will end up chasing abundance but not knowing if you ever have what you really want.

For instance, if you want an abundance of money then how much? How much would an abundance of money be to you?

Subsequently, think about achieving that goal, and having an abundance of what you want. As soon as you do this, you will find that you are getting some negative thoughts, some sense of doubt and uncertainty – you may not believe that you can achieve that goal or have the abundance that you want. Write down the thoughts that come up as you focus on abundance.

Train yourself to eliminate constantly all the negative thoughts about abundance. These are thoughts of doubt, thoughts that say you can't have what you want, and thoughts that lead you to give up. These negative thoughts need to be replaced with positive thoughts about abundance – thoughts that say you can have what you want – thoughts that allow you to succeed and make you want to move forward and pursue your goal. By replacing the negative thoughts with positive thoughts about abundance and success, you begin to develop a positive mindset and you are applying the power of positive thinking to attract abundance.

Positive thinking is not something that you can turn on and off whenever you want. You have to practice positive thinking all the time. And only by doing this every day can you train your mind and direct your subconscious to create more abundance in your life.

Therefore, eliminate the negative thoughts and practice attracting abundance by thinking of all the positive situations that you come across. Take a few moments out of your day and focus on the positive things that happened and the abundant things that exist. Even something as simple as going to work on time is a positive event that you can focus on. Also, focus on all the positive things in your life.

Now, to attract and manifest abundance, go one step further and recognize all the abundance around you. There is an abundance of every-thing in the world. There is an abundance of what you want, but you are just not seeing the abundance because you are probably used to focusing on the lack and limitations. You are most likely always thinking about what you do not have or what is wrong.

Change the way you see things to focus on abundance and begin attracting abundance by seeing the abundance around you. You can think about the simple things like the abundance of air, the abundance of grass, leaves, people, businesses, and money changing hands every day. There truly is an abundance of everything, including what you want. So start seeing abundance everywhere.

Your ability to see abundance has to become automatic for you to attract abundance, as you will only get what you regularly think about. When seeing abundance and being positive are natural, then, changes take place quickly and easily.

Then, you notice that positive thinking makes your life easier and you will enjoy greater abundance when you think about abundance and focus on the positive things that happen every day. Here are some attitude changes that can help you:

- Force yourself to see abundance everywhere;
- The key is to practice every day;
- Start eliminating any negative or limiting thoughts;
- Begin being more confident;
- Decide what abundance means to you.

Play this game with yourself daily: Every day, when you catch yourself being negative or saying something negative, change your thoughts imme-diately and replace them with positive thoughts. That way, things will not change overnight, but they will change over time. It will take some time to get used to being positive but once you have a positive thinking mindset in place, you will see dramatic changes because of the power of positive thinking.

Attracting More Money with Positive Thinking

Positive thinking can help you to attract more money. You can apply positive thinking to create financial success. To do so, you have to change your financial outlook, or how you see your finances, and how you view your current relationship with money. Once you apply positive thinking to your financial outlook, you actually have to change the way you see money and, in the process, you change how you handle money. To apply positive thinking to gain financial success, you have to track your thoughts and feelings about money.

If you find that you do not have enough money, then you likely have a negative outlook on money and have a negative financial situation. This kind of negative outlook will lead to difficulties with money, creating more debt, not earning enough, and just letting money slip through your fingers. This is what's known as a negative thinking mindset towards wealth and personal finances. When you have a positive thinking mindset tied to wealth and your personal finances, you attract and make more money, you handle money better, you find easy ways to make money and your wealth continues to grow. So, how do you apply positive thinking to your wealth and personal finances?

To do so, you should control and track your thoughts and feelings about money and your finances – making note of all your limiting or negative thoughts.

If you have thoughts like 'it is difficult to make money', 'I never make any money', 'money never comes to me', 'there are no good ways to make money', 'I do not know how to make money', etc., these are a clear sign that positive thinking is not tied to your personal wealth and finances.

Once you know which thoughts are not working for you, then you can begin changing them. Moreover, by changing them, you begin to apply positive thinking to your financial situation. As you change these negative thoughts to positive thoughts, you begin to believe that you can and will be able to improve your finances and money situation.

Yet, for that to happen and for positive thinking to take hold in your financial situation, you have to really believe the new thoughts. Your mind will put up a fight and resist the new positive thinking pattern that you're trying to apply to your financial situation. To get past this resistance, you have to give your mind additional support and push yourself to continue replacing those negative thoughts about your finances.

Your feeling, beliefs, and thoughts about finances are tied to the past and old negative thinking processes. Any new, positive thinking that is being applied will naturally be rejected at first. Nevertheless, as you continue applying your new positive thinking patterns and add affirmations and visualizations to your daily practice, you will be able to turn your financial situation around and you will begin finding new ways to make more money while managing your money better.

Facing Challenging Times with Positive Thinking

The Universe is in perpetual motion, so is the human being. Therefore, your life will experience challenges. When everything is going right in your life, it is easy to feel good and be positive. However, the real test is when times are challenging and difficult. In that context, do you still maintain the positive thoughts, feelings, and outlook on life?

In many cases, this is where you find more negative thoughts creeping in. However, this is the time when you need the positive thoughts the most: When times are tough.

Perhaps you have lost your job and job opportunities are bleak, the economic conditions are tough, you have just separated from your partner, etc. It is very easy to have negative thoughts and self-pity, or to go through negative scenarios in your mind and be pulled into a vicious cycle of concerns, fears, worries and anticipation of more problems. In that mood, you can only attract similar conditions.

As positive as you may be when times are good, it is when you face these challenging times that you may forget everything that you have learned, read about on staying positive, and simply focus on the issues and problems instead of focusing on solutions and looking out for opportunities that can help your situation.

When you start on this path, feelings of helplessness, self-pity, resentment, anger, and sadness or depression will follow. You may blame everyone else around you for your predicament, except yourself. Often, this blame will be towards those that are closest to you; you may resent people around you who are successful and cheerful; you may indulge in self-pity to the point that you end up depressed and feeling sad and helpless and cannot focus at all on any solutions. Simply, you will develop a negative attitude towards life.

Sometimes this ends up being a catch as the negative attitude will simply attract more situations that are negative and you basically are digging yourself deeper and deeper into the world of negativity. When you are in this world, even when positive things happen to you or potential opportunities come your way, you may not even see them, as you are not open to looking out for positive opportunities.

There are people out there who complain about everything in their lives and see no joy in their day-to-day living. They miss that spark that passion for life, as their negativity takes over every aspect of their life. Often, these are the people who allow negativity to become central in their lives. Is this the way you want to become? Many are so deeply rooted in their negativity that it is inherent in their nature. This is a sad situation as no one wants to live life this way while there is so much to cherish, enjoy, and appreciate in life.

When you have the right attitude, you can experience all these joys. Now you need to ask yourself; what good is this attitude? Is it helping you to get out of your current situation or is it pulling you deeper into more and more problems and negative feelings?

Keep in mind, that when you think positively about solutions, your subconscious mind will look for solutions. On the other hand, if you simply allow all the negative thoughts to enter your mind, you cause your subconscious mind to create more problems.

Yet, to change your thoughts, you cannot simply snap your fingers and say, 'now I am only thinking positive thoughts,' as the negative ones will keep creeping in and have you further dwell on your issues or circumstances. You must perform actions in order to make any changes. Remember that there is always a solution.

You may need to learn a different skill, accept a different position that may be at a lower level than your previous positions, cut back on your spending habits temporarily, seek alternative therapies, etc.

Often, repeating positive affirmations and visualizations over-and-over again will also help you change your negative thought patterns. Take a walk each day and repeat these affirmations to yourself repeatedly.

By doing this, you are simply reprogramming your subconscious mind and, in simple terms, you are changing your thoughts.

The key is that you are doing something to help your situation. You never know what these actions may lead to. Many times, opportunities come to us indirectly and it is only by keeping an open mind that we try different options. Often, the key is to focus on the present and the future and to forget the past. It is only by forgetting the past that we allow ourselves to focus on the present.

In summary, here is what you need to do when you are facing difficult or challenging times:

- Consciously keep a positive mental attitude all the time;
- Be ready to explore alternatives by keeping an open mind for any opportunities that come your way directly or indirectly;
- Forget the past, this is not something you can change so, instead, simply focus on the present and build the future;
- Use affirmations and visualizations daily to help change your negative thoughts into positive ones;
- Protect and control your environment to connect with positive and experienced people that can help you;
- Apply these steps now and you'll see changes down the road.

Positive thinking is fun and easy to begin applying; so, start changing and eliminating those negative thoughts now and watch your results!

One of the pillars of success, abundance, prosperity, and wealth is knowing how to identify and choose the people in your circle, as we have already mentioned. Your entourage and your environment influence your life and your way of thinking and therefore your results.

In the next chapter, we are going to talk about how to choose the people around us to create assured success, abundance, prosperity, and wealth.

Chapter 12

Use the Power of the Mastermind

How do you create your 'dream team' or 'success team' in an intelligent way? Napoleon Hill[10] calls this group of individuals: "Mastermind alliance". According to the Holy Bible, "He that walketh with wise men shall be wise: But a companion of fools shall be destroyed" (*Proverbs 13:20*, King James Bible).

The human being is a social animal, which is why we need to inter-act with other humans to achieve our goals or objectives in ways that are beneficial to all. However, in the process of diligent selection of individuals, as in other success processes, it is necessary to apply principles that work and have been proven for centuries. Chance, common sense, and emotion have no place. Jesus used similar principles to select and choose His twelve apostles, which enabled Him to achieve the goals we all know. The Holy Bible said, "But Jesus told him, let the dead bury their own dead. You, however, go and proclaim the kingdom of God" (*Luke 9:60*, Berean Study Bible).

The 'dream team' or 'success team' is the set of individuals, organizations, or any system, that is useful in achieving and reaching our goals at the scale of excellence we want. Our activities take place in a global world; as a result, individuals or organizations do not need to be located on the same worksite, they can even be virtual that means they can be people who you have never met in person but only connect with virtually through the Internet.

---

10. Hill, Napoleon (1937). *Think and Grow Rich*. Chicago, Illinois: Combined Registry Company.

When the right people have been chosen, and work in harmony on clear and precise goals, their interactions create and develop a form of job-related intelligence that I call the 'collective intelligence', which motivates and stimulates them to create or provide more and better services or products than if each of these people relied solely on their own means and resources to achieve the same goals. There is also the benefit of the effect of the expression: "There is strength in numbers". I will comment on this saying by stating only that it is the disciplined and controlled unity that is the strength. Indeed, in the field of psychology, it is shown that the environment, including the entities in the environment, influences the development of the individual as well as his or her intelligence. This influence can be positive and productive or negative and destructive; hence, the importance of the need to use principles of success in the process of creating our successful team.

History tells us that many organizations have dissolved because of the poor selection of key people. On the other hand, some successful people have lost everything and even gone bankrupt for selecting bad associates whom they had the misfortune to meet on the way to their success. In this chapter, we will use principles that work to create our success team.

Designing a successful team is not a job that must be done in a hurry; understand that you do not need anyone else to succeed. The only person you need first is yourself, and your developed awareness of success that you continue to improve in order to reach your full potential. Then, if other people can help you expand your prosperity, it's very welcome, because all the great people who are successful have always collaborated with others at one moment during the expansion of their wealth. There may be some exceptions to what has just been said, though if you look closely you will find that if a group starts and succeeds, it is actually a team of successful individuals with individually successful abilities similar to what we find in a successful team.

When selecting individuals for your success team, I identify three types of people; I assume here that these people have good human qualities, competence, experience, and convincing results:

1. People who represent an extension of your skills;
2. People who bring complementary skills;
3. People who are your advisors.

People Who Extend Your Skills

These people bring the expertise you do not have or you do not want to practice. The largest number of your associates must come from this category. They provide expanded knowledge and skills.

People Who Complement Your Skills

These people have similar expertise to yours. Usually, it's a person or two, depending on your activities. This person can replace you in case of absence.

Your Advisers, Mentors, or Coaches

These wise people may be living or may have left a legacy of knowledge through books, recordings, etc.; they have proven by their outstanding results that they are exceptional human beings.

Pay special attention to people who are no longer living; these people still exist in the spirit. Most often, they have left writings that we can use to advance in our lives. We can even invoke their spirit to guide us in certain circumstances. It is not only Jesus Christ that we can invoke, when needed.

You need to assess their results, enthusiasm, and determination, as well as other skills related to your work environment. It is wise to identify the principles of success that these people used to achieve their goals because one does not succeed by chance, nor by using only common sense or emotions. Successful people require guides, as the captain of the boat uses a compass or GPS to navigate. I have an expression that I often use: "Never leave opportunity to chance".

Some people are so conditioned for failure that, when you suggest a valuable idea to them, instead of trying to test it for themselves or validate and verify that idea with a person who can confirm its value with facts and convincing experience, they will simply address people who do not know anything about it or who have not created something relevant in their lives. I have often met this type of people. If you bring this type of people into your team, you can imagine the future of your business. They behave this way unconsciously; they do not even know that they are conditioned for mediocrity.

Take an example: If you are putting together a financial package to invest in building three-hundred homes, there is no point in going to seek advice from a person unable to pay his or her rent each month. The smart approach is to consult a person who has already invested in a building of three hundred homes or better five hundred units and more. This person has developed an expertise that will help you more than you can imagine. And your success will be assured.

Remember that, when a serious company wants to hire an employee for example, they conduct several job interviews to select the best person. You too, do the same thing for your success.

Bear in mind that the goal of taking all these precautions in advance is to prepare ourselves for success using the principles of success. Most of the challenges we encounter in our activities, others have already encountered and overcome. Therefore, when using principles, we automatically avoid these challenges without conscious effort, which allows us to produce more in a very short time.

By choosing the right people for your success team and working in harmony, you will move from simple cooperation to the mastermind alliance spirit that achieves absolutely exceptional results.

Remember, throughout this selection process for building your success team, that there are not two captains in a boat. You are the captain and you choose your crew to cross the ocean of business, which can be tumultuous, and arrive safely. However, you are not choosing people to think for you.

Personal Examples

I created several companies with collaborators and all these companies were failures and the main reason resides in the selection of collaborators. Since I did not have the chance to have on-hand a book like the one you are reading now, my only selection criteria were:

1. They are friends;
2. I loved them;
3. They wanted to do business with me;
4. I wanted to help them;
5. I wanted to please them;
6. etc.

In addition, I provided the core funding. Under these conditions, it was easy for anyone to do business with me. But, everything ended in frustration and dissatisfaction – founded or fabricated. And most importantly, everyone was right. These people were bad choices because I did not apply the mastermind alliance principal and did not check anything.

If you read or re-read what is written in this chapter, and even this book, you can easily conclude beyond a shadow of a doubt that not all of these companies can survive or be successful. And you will also straightforwardly understand why I am in a position to be able to tell you to choose your partners wisely. I speak from real life experiences.

What Do Others Think of You?

Believe in yourself; work strategically to do well what you want to do. Use the principles of success. Learn constantly and do not care what others think about you – especially people who have never proven anything in their life. Jesus says it very well, "Let the dead bury their own dead" (*Luke 9:60*, Berean Study Bible).

It's what you think of yourself that will move you forward to succeed – not to be confused with positive suggestions for continuous improvement that allow you to improve.

I had been raised to believe that you should not disturb others; you had to please everyone in order to please God. This mentality discourages us from evaluating anyone. Although we sometimes do an assessment, we do not do it the right way or rigorously. This logically explains our results.

The certainty is that business, as well as our goals in life, are not games. We must know what we want, measure the associated risks, and decide, regardless of the opinion of others. Here, we must not neglect doing our due diligence. Before deciding, use all available knowledge to make an appropriate decision. And, if no knowledge exists, we have the privilege of returning to the Universe to guide us, because our good desire is a divine desire to help us and others. The world is full of wonders that some people claim to be impossible at the time. For example, Napoleon Hill[11] said that, to create the first V8 engine, Henry Ford doggedly insisted on telling his engineers to build the new engine that they thought was impossible before they found the design method of the V8 car. Henry Ford demonstrated tremendous persistence and faith. How many of us stop at the first sign of an obstacle or the first opposition or difficulty in carrying out actions to fulfill our desires? Know that success smiles to those who do not stop at the first opposition or obstacle.

There are people who make decisions without using the information, knowledge, and facts available. Then, they make expensive mistakes and

11. Hill, Napoleon, Stone, W. Clement (1991). *Success Through A Positive Mental Attitude*, Pocket Books

lose. I call this 'negligence' because these people do not learn anything from this type of error.

Monitoring the Results of Team Members

There is no point in spending time consciously choosing associates and then leaving them to their own devices while hoping for exceptional results. Throughout this book, many ideas often appear, but mainly: Discipline, control, analysis, and verification.

We all live in a dynamic and changing world, which is very good – otherwise, it would be monotonous. You cannot change this law. All you can do is use it to your favor and for your success. The human being also changes consciously sometimes; other times unconsciously. You must, therefore, train your staff and then monitor, analyze, and constantly check their results. The period of these audits varies widely, depending on the projects and the areas of activity. This can be by day, week, month, quarter, etc. Follow the practices in your area of activity. If this is not available, or in doubt, just test out periods until you find the time that best suits your activities and the risks attached to them.

For example, in the field of property rental management, monitoring can be done daily or weekly in the case of hotel management; monthly, in the case of the management of residential or commercial buildings. However, in the transport sector, monitoring can be done daily. As you can see, there are no exact formulas applicable in all areas; however, by testing your market and consulting other professionals in your industry, you will be able to easily identify effective follow-up periods without compromising the smooth running of your business.

Note that monitoring does not only concern your team members – you, too, are part of the follow-up.

The follow-up process should not be questionable and suspicious or involve spying on individuals. Establish clear, measurable, and controllable criteria for all; then, evolve these criteria constantly, according to the challenges of the job. Employees can participate in the development of the monitoring criteria.

Personally, as I already mentioned, I evaluate myself systematically at the end of each action, interaction, or transaction. I made this an automatic habit as a result – I do it without thinking about it and without effort.

Conclusion

The key to success in using the powers of the mind is repetition; let me repeat it again here because this aspect is really important and represents one of the essential bases of any profound and lasting change. To do this, read and reread this book on a regular basis until you get the desired results.

And you too, like me, could say that we become what we think about most of the time and that the powers of the mind can transform our life and our future, the lives of our family, our loved ones, the people we love, and others, so be it.

I wish you peace, love, joy, abundance, prosperity, wealth, health, security, a lot of money, as well as divine blessings!

Afterword by Peggy McColl

Every now and then, I read a book that truly inspires me. This is exactly what Rémi has achieved with *Practice Getting Rich for a Better Life*.

Not only does the author inspire you to change your thinking, but he also takes it one step further and inspires you to take the action to make it happen. This book is filled with ideas and techniques that can be applied in our everyday life whether at home or at work. These techniques have been proven to create success, happiness, and satisfaction to those who have implemented them.

The biggest lesson we can take away from reading this book is that what we are thinking makes the difference between success and failure. What makes the biggest difference between people who achieve their goals versus those that do not, is their mindset.

"Before you become a millionaire, you must learn to think like one" (Dr. Thomas Stanley).

But Rémi has also taught us that thinking and feeling alone will not bring you all you desire; you also need to set goals that are actionable and accomplishable. You can think positively all day long, but without knowing how to set the right kind of goals, you won't get there. Rémi understands this and has given you the knowledge to not only set attainable goals but also actually accomplish them.

In Rémi's words, *"All wealth comes from within – spirit. This book teaches you step-by-step to combine external and internal actions to create stable wealth."*

Rémi explained how you really can use the power of positive thinking to create the financial success, affluence, and prosperity you deserve.

Most people never experience the wealth and abundance they could have because they never learn how to change the way they think and they know nothing of the importance of having the proper money mindset to achieve those things.

Rémi demonstrates the power of faith in action. With the practical techniques outlined in this book, you can energize your life – and give yourself the initiative needed to carry out your ambitions, hopes and dreams.

Therefore, the bottom line is this:

- Expand your vision, embrace your challenges, and use adversity as a springboard to achieving massive success;

- Only surround yourself with positive people and ignore those that make you doubt yourself;

- Use your imagination to create and achieve all that you want. You have more in you than you will ever exhaust in your lifetime;

- If you believe you can achieve it, then chances are you will achieve it (whatever it is). Similarly, if you set your mind to doing something attainable, the probability of getting it done is very high;

- All of us want to achieve something great… whether it's financial, relationship, happiness, peace, etc, and now that you have an understanding of what you need to focus on, only you can stop you from being successful;

- The time for thinking negatively or small for fear of failure is in your past.

You now possess the tools and techniques that will help you change your thinking and learn exactly how to apply it to your own life so that you can achieve success in all your goals and create the life you want.

Peggy McColl
New York Times bestselling author

Suggested reading

I have read many books over the years. I propose here a list of the principal works, which I consult often. There is no preference, priority, or order of importance in this list:

The Holy Bible

Think and Grow Rich, Napoleon Hill

The Science of Getting Rich, Wallace D. Wattles

The Master Key, Charles Francis Haanel

The Power of Focus, Jack Canfield, Mark Victor Hansen, and Les Hewitt

You Were Born Rich, Bob Proctor

Contact

Website link

https://practicegettingrich.com/

https://remiwognin.com/

Where to buy the book

https://practicegettingrich.com/

Upcoming books

https://askbelieveactreceive.com/

https://thinkserveandgrowrich.com/

Email address

support@remiwognin.com

About the Author

Rémi Wognin, author, consultant, and personal development advisor, lives in Montreal, Canada, and travels very often to the United States. He describes in this book, very powerful, practical techniques that can transform the reality and the life of any person who uses them systematically and persistently.

These techniques, whose origins are very ancient, have changed the lives of many people and allowed them to move from being someone who lives on a salary week-to-week to a person who decides what he or she wants every month or every year, and under what conditions. Your external environment is always a reflection of your inner world. It is therefore with great pleasure and enthusiasm that he shares his findings and experience with the world for a more prosperous and rich world.

Giving a Voice to Creativity!

Wouldn't you love to help the physically, spiritually, and mentally challenged?

Would you like to make a difference in a child's life?

Imagine giving them: confidence; self-esteem; pride; and self-respect. Perhaps a legacy that lives on.

You see, that's what we do. We give a voice to the creativity in their hearts, for those who would otherwise not be heard.

Join us by going to

HeartstobeHeard.com

Help us, help others.

Made in the USA
Monee, IL
02 March 2022

92128289R00080